Discover
Britain's
historic
Wales
houses

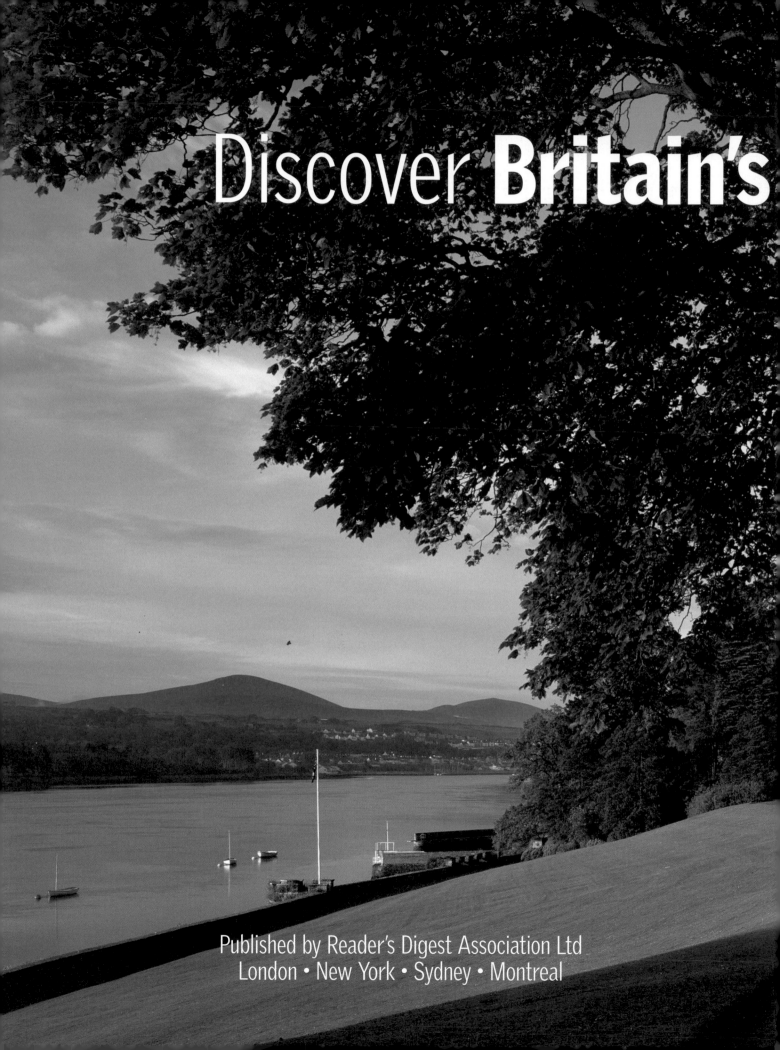

Discover Britain's

Published by Reader's Digest Association Ltd
London • New York • Sydney • Montreal

historic houses

Wales

Simon Jenkins

Contents

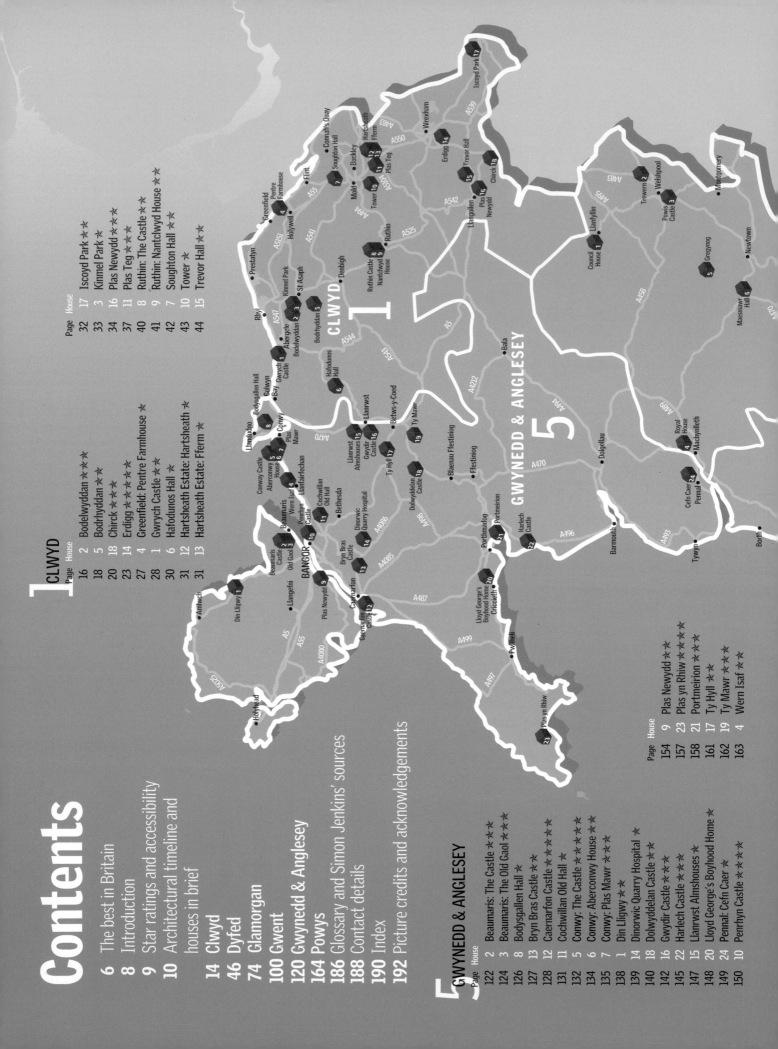

1 CLWYD

5 GWYNEDD & ANGLESEY

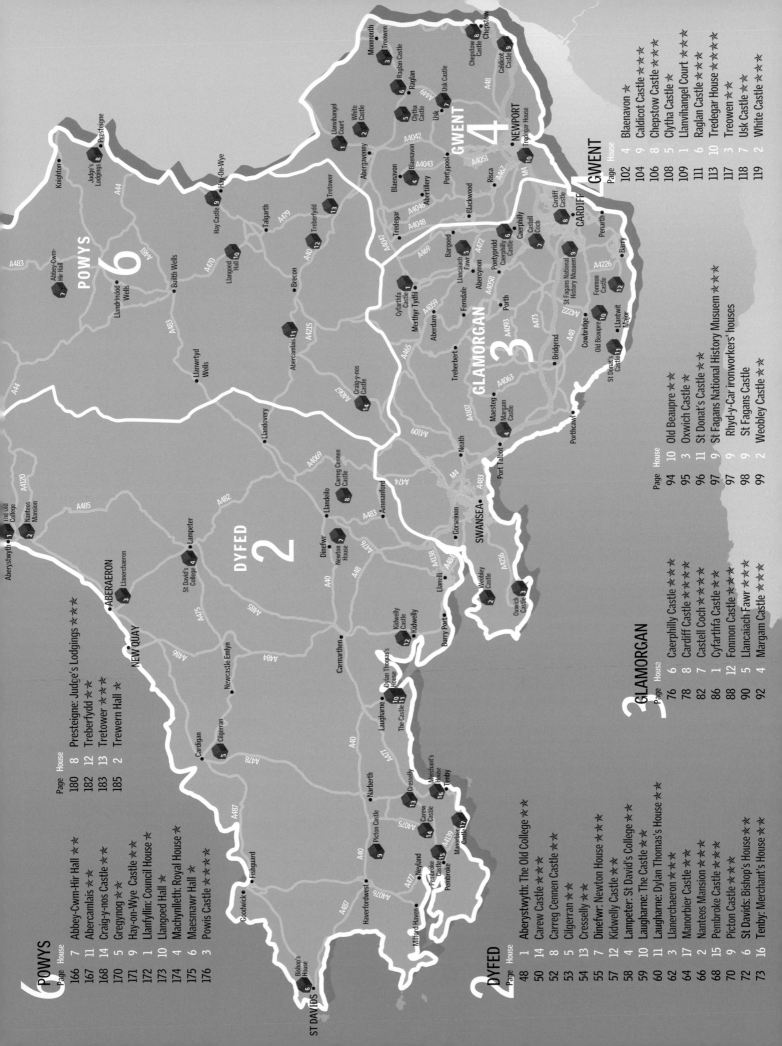

The best in Britain

SCOTLAND

114	Abbotsford, Melrose	
127	Blair Castle	
130	Cawdor Castle	
128	Craigievar Castle	
112	Drumlanrig Castle	
131	Dunrobin Castle	
129	Dunvegan Castle	

126	Glamis Castle	
120	Hill House	
121	Hopetoun House	
124	Inveraray Castle	
117	Manderston	
115	Mellerstain	
118	Mount Stuart	
119	New Lanark	
122	Palace of Holyroodhouse	
125	Scone Palace	
132	Skara Brae	
123	Stirling Castle	
116	Thirlestane Castle	
113	Traquair House	

22	Hever Castle		61	Canons Ashby	
80	Holkham Hall		102	Castle Howard	
37	Home House		14	Charleston	
79	Houghton Hall		54	Chastleton	
107	Hutton-in-the-Forest		91	Chatsworth House	
25	Ightham Mote		111	Chillingham Castle	
74	Kedleston Hall		36	Chiswick House	
21	Kensington Palace		56	Claydon House	
5	Kingston Lacy		16	Cothay Manor	
50	Knebworth House		109	Cragside	
24	Knole		70	Deene Park	
29	Lacock Abbey		38	Dennis Severs House	
1	Lanhydrock		28	Dyrham Park	
26	Leeds Castle		52	Eastnor Castle	
104	Levens Hall		40	Eltham Palace	
19	Longleat		100	Fairfax House	
89	Lyme Park		13	Firle Place	
53	Madresfield Court		3	Forde Abbey	
48	Magdalen College		27	Godinton Park	
17	Montacute House		8	Goodwood House	
101	Newby Hall		78	Grimsthorpe Castle	
94	Newstead Abbey		90	Haddon Hall	
96	Nostell Priory		66	Hagley Hall	
6	Osborne House		35	Ham House	
32	Osterley Park		34	Hampton Court	
72	Oxburgh Hall		93	Hardwick Hall	
10	Parham House		98	Harewood House	
23	Penshurst Place		76	Harlaxton Manor	
9	Petworth House		65	Harvington Hall	
106	Raby Castle		51	Hatfield House	
59	Ragley Hall				
41	Restoration House				

ORKNEY

132

WESTERN ISLES

129

HIGHLAND

131

130 MORAY

Aberdeen

ABERDEENSHIRE

128

ANGUS

Dundee

126

SCOTLAND

PERTH & KINROSS

125

127

FIFE

Edinburgh

EAST LOTHIAN

116

117

115

114

113

SCOTTISH BORDERS

123 STIRLING

FALKIRK

WEST LOTHIAN

MID LOTHIAN

122

121

119

LANARKSHIRE

112

DUMFRIES AND GALLOWAY

Glasgow

120

ARGYLLSHIRE

124

BUTESHIRE

118

AYRSHIRE

NORTHUMBERLAND

111

110

109

108

Newcastle upon Tyne

Sunderland

WALES

Caernarfon Castle ✱	82
Cardiff Castle ✱	43
Castell Coch ✱	42
Conwy Castle ✱	86
Erddig ✱	87
Penrhyn Castle ✱	84
Plas Mawr ✱	85
Plas Newydd ✱	83
Powis Castle ✱	73
Raglan Castle	45
Tredegar House ✱	44

ENGLAND

Alnwick Castle	110
Althorp	62
Arbury Hall	68
Arundel Castle	11
Astley Hall	95
Athelhampton House	4
Audley End	58
Bateman's	15
Belton House	77
Belvoir Castle	75
Beningbrough Hall	99
Berkeley Castle	46
Blenheim Palace	47
Blickling Hall	81
Bolsover Castle	92
Boughton House	69
Brighton Pavilion	12
Broughton Castle	55
Burghley House	71
Burton Agnes Hall	103
Burton Constable Hall	97

Saltram House	2
Sherborne Castle	18
Sizergh Castle	105
Speke Hall	88
Spencer House	39
St John's College	63
Syon House	33
The Vyne	30
Trinity College	64
Uppark	7
Waddesdon Manor	49

Wallington Hall	108
Warwick Castle	60
Wightwick Manor	67
Wilton House	20
Windsor Castle	31
Woburn Abbey	57

5 Star
4 Star
✱ Featured in this book

Historic houses of Wales

Clwyd (comprising most of Conwy, Denbighshire and Flintshire) has been dubbed the Welsh Tuscany for its rolling hills and secret valleys. This has always been border country and through the Middle Ages armies marched back and forth to wars in Gwynedd to the west. Edward I left castles at Ruthin and Rhuddlan and the Mortimers built a fortress at Chirk.

The Jacobeans were spectacular at Plas Teg, while 17th-century domestic building was epitomised by Erddig, now immaculately presented by the National Trust. Clwyd owes little that is visible to the Georgians, although the 'ladies of Llangollen' left eccentric Plas Newydd. In the 19th century Clwyd found its stride on the strength of English wealth. Bodelwyddan and Gwrych Castle are castellated Regency at its most extraordinary. Sir Gilbert Scott brought High Gothic to Hafodunos and Eden Nesfield's Queen Anne revival can be seen at Kinmel and in his additions at Bodrhyddan.

The ancient Welsh kingdom of Deheubarth evolved from that of **Dyfed** (Carmarthenshire, Pembrokeshire, Ceredigion) in the 10th century. By the time of William the Conqueror's visit to St David's shrine in 1081, it was a Christian society some five centuries old. William reached an understanding of autonomy with the king of Deheubarth, Rhys ap Tewdwr, whose capital was at Dinefwr, but this changed under William's son, William Rufus. In 1190 the Montgomerys swept south through Powys and Ceredigion to the coast at Pembroke. English and Flemish colonists were imported and southern Pembrokeshire so thoroughly 'cleansed' of Welsh as to be known as 'little England beyond Wales', its language and place names English to this day.

This Norman conquest produced castles second only to Gwynedd in scale. Pembroke's great keep was built in the early 12th century. There followed Carreg Cennen, Cilgerran, Kidwelly, Carew, Laugharne and Manorbier, the last being the birthplace of Gerald of Wales. Henry Tudor was born and raised in Pembroke Castle and his courtiers converted Carew and Manorbier to sumptuous Elizabethan houses. The merchant's house at Tenby recalls Tudor entrepreneurs. The Georgians left comfortable houses at Dinefwr and Llanerchaeron, and in the stylish conversion of Picton Castle. Good rococo interiors can be found at Cresselly and Nanteos. Dyfed's most prominent Victorian relic was the great hotel constructed in 1864 at Aberystwyth, swiftly converted into the University of Wales.

Glamorgan is Wales's home county, with almost half the country's population. Its mineral exports made it the richest county in Britain in Victorian days, which made its 20th-century decline all the more drastic. In the 21st century Cardiff has prospered, aided by devolution.

The Normans built an early castle at Cardiff, which survives. Llewelyn's revolt led to the construction in 1268 of the great castle at Caerphilly, predating those of Edward I in the north. Tudor building can be seen at Llancaiach Fawr and St Fagans Castle, and at St Donat's. From the 18th century, the Orangery at Margam and rococo saloon at Fonmon are exceptional.

In 1760 the use of coking coal rather than charcoal to work iron set off a 'black gold rush' to Glamorgan. Workers poured in from the countryside, making Merthyr Tydfil the first industrial town in Britain where English was not the language of the streets. The industrial kings of Merthyr were the Crawshays, who built the Regency mansion of Cyfarthfa Castle. Otherwise, virtually all traces of this boom have vanished. The best effort to recall them is at Blaenavon in Gwent. In the Victorian era the 3rd Marquess of Bute inherited extensive Herbert land and used his wealth to build Cardiff docks and two of the most spectacular gothic revival palaces in Europe, Cardiff Castle and Castell Coch.

As the 'gateway to Wales', **Gwent** was always vulnerable to invasion. There are Roman villas aplenty and it was swiftly subdued by the Normans: Chepstow Castle, begun the year after Hastings, was the first of 25 Norman castles there. They and their successors form a fine collection: White for isolation, Raglan for pomp, Caldicote for size, Usk for endearing ruination. The county was anglicised by Henry VIII as Monmouthshire and not 'returned' to Wales until 1974. Elizabethan and Jacobean manors survive at Llanvihangel and Treowen. The Restoration is superbly represented at Tredegar.

Gwynedd (Merionedd, Caernarfon, parts of Conwy) is the heart, if not always the head, of Wales. It is the most remote, most mountainous, least conquered and most 'pure' province and formed the backbone of the rebellions of Llywelyn and Glyndwr in the late-13th and early-15th centuries. Llywelyn's castle survives at Dolwyddelan. It is overshadowed by Caernarfon, Conwy and Harlech, works of Edward I's master-builder, James of St George. Edward settled English boroughs round his castles, of which Conwy is today the most complete.

The Tudor ascendancy has left two of the finest 16th-century town houses in Britain, Plas Mawr and Aberconwy. Gwydir is a medieval mansion. The county's prosperity from slate and minerals is displayed in the 19th-century houses along the north coast. Pre-eminent is the massive pile of Penrhyn by Thomas Hopper outside Bangor. Herbert North's Wern Isaf is a rare Welsh example of Arts and Crafts style. Finally, glowing on the north shore of Cardigan Bay is Portmeirion, a delightful essay in 20th-century Welsh picturesque by Clough Williams Ellis.

Anglesey, or Ynys Mon, is steeped in the romance of Wales's pre-history, meriting the title of 'Mam Cymru', mother of Wales. Pre-Celtic remains dot the landscape and later the island was a centre of druidic worship. This was the last place in Wales to defy the Romans. At Din Lligwy pre-history merges into the Celtic era.

Anglesey was the redoubt of the Llywelyns, its cornfields supplying Welsh armies in their fight against the English. In response Edward I settled one of his most impressive castles and boroughs at Beaumaris, today a picturesque Georgian town. Plas Newydd, gothick in style and beautifully situated on the Menai Straits, is notable for its mural by Rex Whistler.

Powys (Breconshire, Radnorshire, Montgomeryshire) emerged as a kingdom as the advancing Saxons pushed the Welsh back into the Cambrian mountains. The Saxon king, Offa of Mercia, erected a dyke to mark what has formed the roughly agreed boundary between England and Wales to this day. The Normans showed no such tact. In 1086 Roger of Montgomery pushed west towards the sea, dividing north from south Wales. Present-day Powys still meets tidal water at Machynlleth.

The modern county is a soft landscape of hills, old villages and small churches. The Tudors brought Powys, the grandest house in Wales, now the refashioned Powis Castle. Other Tudor buildings survive in the remarkable complex at Tretower and in the 'border black-and-white' of Trewern and Maesmawr. The Georgians are evidenced at Abercamlais and the judges lodgings at Presteigne. The Victorians were riotous at Adeline Patti's Craig-y-nos retreat and sober at the model country estates at Leighton and Treberfydd.

Simon Jenkins

☆ STAR RATINGS AND ACCESSIBILITY ☆☆☆☆

The 'star' rating system was first devised for and used in *England's Thousand Best Houses*. They rate the overall quality of a house as presented to the public, and not gardens or other attractions. On balance houses, however famous, have been scaled down for not being easily accessible or for being only partly open.

The top rating, five stars, is given to those houses that qualify as 'international' celebrities. Four stars are awarded to houses of outstanding architectural quality and public display. Three-star houses comprise the run of good historic houses, well displayed and worthy of national

promotion. Two and one-star houses are of more local interest, are hard to visit, or have just one significant feature.

Accessibility varies greatly, from buildings that are open all year to houses that can only be visited 'by appointment' (rarely, I have included a private property that is not open at all, but is viewable from nearby walks or public gardens). Opening hours tend to alter from year to year, but an indication of how accessible a house is to visitors is given at the start of each entry, together with brief information on location and ownership. Many of the houses are now National Trust or Cadw

properties, some are now museums or hotels, others are privately owned by families who open to the public for part of the year. Some owners, understandably, seek to cluster visitors on particular days. More details for each house are given at the back of the book, and readers are advised to check before visiting.

A final note, houses are, or should be, living things subject to constant change and how we view them is bound to be a subject of debate. I welcome any correction or comment, especially from house owners, sent to me c/o the publisher.

NOTE: On pages 6-7 the 4 and 5-star houses in Scotland were selected by Hamish Scott and the editors of Reader's Digest.

Architectural timeline
and the houses of Wales in brief

Abbey-cwm-hir
A Victorian mansion, with steeply pitched roofs and gothic features, built on the site of a once-great Cistercian abbey.

Abercamlais
A Georgian house of c1710, built round an earlier farmhouse. An unusual dovecote straddles a stream in the grounds.

Aberystwyth: The Old College
Built as a hotel on the town's sea front and designed by neo-gothic J. P. Seddon, who also supervised its conversion to a college.

Beaumaris Castle
Begun in 1295 by Master James of St George to be Edward I's headquarters, but never completed.

Beaumaris: The Old Gaol
A prison designed in response to the 1823 Gaol Act, and including such innovations as an infirmary, washroom and nursery.

Blaenavon
Two cottages, once the homes of 18th-century ironworkers, one reconstructed as the home of a foreman, the other as a poor worker's home.

Bodelwyddan
Mansion rebuilt in the 1830s in castellated gothic style. The Arts-and-Crafts interiors were revived in the 1980s when the house was taken over by the National Portrait Gallery.

Bodrhyddan
Medieval house rebuilt in 1696 and extended in 1872 in Anglo-Dutch revival style. The William-and-Mary façade can still be seen.

Bodysgallen Hall
Jacobean mansion built around a tower house that probably once served as a watchtower. It was rebuilt in c1620 to a medieval plan.

Bryn Bras Castle
Country house built in the 1820s in a neo-Norman style, complete with a towered keep and arcade of Norman arches.

Caernarfon Castle
Castle built in 1282 after Edward I's defeat of Llywelyn. It was reinforced in the 1290s, after succumbing to an attack, and was sufficiently strengthened to withstand Glyndwr's forces.

Caerphilly Castle
The castle of a Marcher lord, built in 1268. Sited on flat land, it was protected by two moats, two gatehouses and two curtain walls

Caldicot Castle
An early Marcher castle on the site of a Norman motte, extended in the 14th century and converted into a residence in the 1880s.

Cardiff Castle
A site comprising an original Norman castle, a Georgian house and a stunning gothic revival palace, begun by William Burges in 1865.

Carew Castle
Probably first built c1100, Carew was fortified in the 14th century then transformed in the 16th into an Elizabethan prodigy house.

Carreg Cennen Castle
Picturesque ruin of a Norman castle on a rocky outcrop, possibly once a Roman site. The castle was rebuilt in the late 13th century but demolished by Yorkists in 1462.

Castell Coch
Gothic-style Victorian fantasy castle built for the Marquess of Bute by William Burges at the same time as Cardiff Castle. The lavish interiors evoke medieval art and architecture.

Chepstow Castle
Begun in 1067, this was the first castle built by the Normans in the Welsh Marches – the keep was one of the first stone castles in Britain. It was extended in the 13th century.

Chirk
The castle of a Marcher lord, Robert Mortimer, built in the late 13th or early 14th century. Acquired by the Middletons who added rooms and apartments in the ensuing centuries.

Cilgerran
Believed to be on the site of one of Gerald of Wales' castles, Cilgerran was rebuilt in the 13th century and withstood an attack by Glyndwr before falling into ruin.

Clytha Castle
A banqueting house hill-top folly, with castellated turrets and fake towers, built in loving memory of a deceased wife.

Cochwillan Old Hall
A Great Hall of the 1450s, built in the courtyard of a medieval house, with a fine hammerbeam roof and well-carved frieze.

Conwy Castle
A stunning Edward I castle begun at the same time as Caernarfon by Master James of St George. The outer walls and towers have survived particularly well.

Conwy: Aberconwy House
A merchants house from the mid 16th century, with parts possibly dating to the 13th. The basement and raised ground floor levels are stone, with timbered upper storeys.

Conwy: Plas Mawr
A grand mansion built in 1576 by a former ambassador to Bruges. The interiors feature extraordinary surviving plasterwork, some painted in original Tudor colours.

Craig-y-nos Castle
An early Victorian house extended in 1878 by singer Adelina Patti in Scots-baronial style. A mini opera house was added in the 1880s.

Cresselly
An Adam-style mansion by architect William Thomas of Pembroke. The Georgian façade was extended by two flanking Victorian wings.

Cyfartha Castle
A grey stone mansion in Regency castellated style, built in 1824–5 opposite the Merthyr ironworks that funded its construction. The round drawing room features Adam wallpaper.

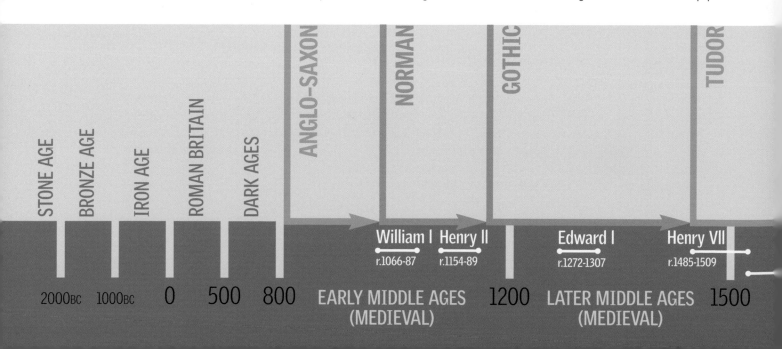

STONE AGE | BRONZE AGE | IRON AGE | ROMAN BRITAIN | DARK AGES | ANGLO–SAXON | NORMAN | GOTHIC | TUDOR

William I r.1066-87   Henry II r.1154-89   Edward I r.1272-1307   Henry VII r.1485-1509

2000BC 1000BC 0 500 800 EARLY MIDDLE AGES (MEDIEVAL) 1200 LATER MIDDLE AGES (MEDIEVAL) 1500

Din Lligwy
Remains of a settlement dating back to late Roman times. The walls of some huts survive, as do the walls that surrounded the village.

Dinefwr
The park includes the ruins of a Norman castle and a Restoration mansion, Newton House, remodelled in the 1770s and in the 1850s.

Dinorwic Quarry Hospital
An early Victorian hospital for injured slate miners, overlooking Lake Padarn. The original wards and some medical equipment survive.

Dolwyddelan Castle
Stronghold of Llywelyn the Great, probably built by the Welsh prince c1200. The keep survives with the Great Chamber still roofed.

Erdigg
House built in 1682 in Restoration style with a modest external façade but exceptionally fine interiors, some with Georgian additions.

Fonmon Castle
Fortified tower house, with the hall on the first floor. A wing was added in the Restoration and the interiors redecorated in the 1760s.

Greenfield: Pentre Farmhouse
A hall house built in the 16th century, and altered over the centuries. It was moved to the museum in 1983 and rebuilt as in the 1600s.

Gregynog Hall
The reconstruction, begun in 1837, of a 17th-century black-and-white 'magpie' house, but built in concrete. An original Jacobean interior survives.

Gwrych Castle
Ruined remains of a once-magnificent Regency house, built along a hillside in a romantic gothic style.

Gwydir Castle
Medieval house rebuilt c1500, extended and refurbished by Elizabethan and Jacobean owners. The dining room has fine Jacobean panelling, once lost but now happily restored.

Hafodunas Hall
A Victorian gothic house by Sir Gilbert Scott, now a ruined shell. The sculptor John Gibson created decorative reliefs for the interiors, some of which remain.

Medieval castles

After the invasion of 1066, the Normans built castles as part of their campaign to secure their new territories. First, they introduced the motte-and-bailey castle, with a wooden palisade on top of an earth mound and a dry ditch around the base; the bailey was an enclosure at the base of the mound housing the services. These castles could be erected quickly to provide a safe garrison base.

As the Norman lords gained more territory, they established a network of military strongholds, big enough to accommodate troops and large households, and began to build their castles in stone. At the centre was the keep – a fortified tower with apartments within – built in a defendable spot. The keep was surrounded by the inner ward and protected by an outer wall. Further wards with their own defensive walls were sometimes added, linked by fortified gatehouses. Castle design grew in sophistication through the Middle Ages; the concentric castle plan – where the inner ward was surrounded by an outer ward, which in turn was surrounded by a ditch or moat – was used by Edward I as part of his castle building in northern Wales. But castle architecture was to change dramatically following the introduction of gunpowder.

Harlech Castle

Harlech Castle
One of the castles built on a concentric plan by Master James of St George in the 1280s. It fell to Glyndwr in 1404 and became his base.

Hartsheath Estate: Hartsheath
A Regency mansion with glazed Doric porch by architect Charles Mathews in a style reminiscent of John Nash.

Hartsheath Estate: Fferm
A late Elizabethan hall house, missing one wing of its original H-plan, but with original fireplace and chimney in place.

Hay Castle
Of Norman origins, the castle is still the most prominent feature in the 'book town' of Hay. A Jacobean mansion, built against the keep, forms the main part of the castle today.

Iscoyd Park
A house dating from the early 18th century but extended some 40 years later with a new wing. A new portico and dining room were added in the 1840s.

Kidwelly Castle
Norman fortress strengthened in the early 12th century. An outer ward, built around the inner to offer even further protection, was added in the 13th century.

Kinmel Park
Victorian mansion by Eden Nesfield, gutted by fire. Inspired by Hampton Court, Kinmel was built of red brick with stone dressings and white-framed windows.

Lampeter: St David's College
University building in Regency-gothic style, opened in 1822. It is on the 'Oxbridge' model, ranged around a cloistered quadrangle.

Laugharne Castle
Norman castle rebuilt in the late 13th century, then rebuilt again as a mansion in the 16th by Sir John Perrot of Carew.

Laugharne: Dylan Thomas's House
The 19th-century boathouse that was the poet's last home. The sitting room and nearby study are preserved as they were in 1953.

Llancaiach Fawr
A house from the 1530s, when domestic architecture was changing from medieval to Elizabethan in form. The interiors are restored as they would have been during the Civil War.

Llanerchaeron
A villa designed in the early 1790s and built in Regency style, one of Nash's first commissions. The interiors are preserved as they would have been in the early 20th century.

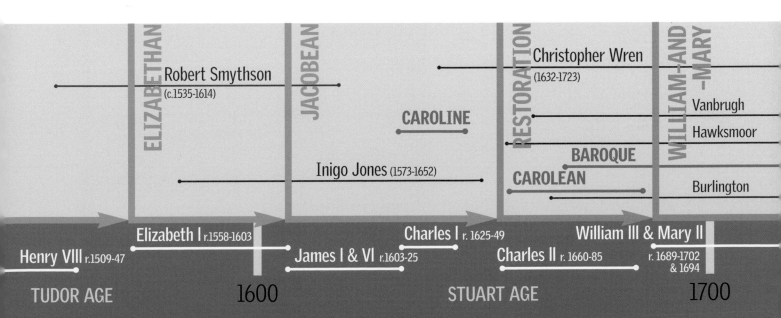

TUDOR AGE 1600 STUART AGE 1700

Henry VIII r.1509-47

Elizabeth I r.1558-1603

James I & VI r.1603-25

Charles I r. 1625-49

Charles II r. 1660-85

William III & Mary II r. 1689-1702 & 1694

ELIZABETHAN — Robert Smythson (c.1535-1614)

JACOBEAN

CAROLINE

Inigo Jones (1573-1652)

RESTORATION — Christopher Wren (1632-1723)

Vanbrugh

Hawksmoor

BAROQUE

CAROLEAN

Burlington

WILLIAM-AND-MARY

William Burges (1827-1881)

Burges began his career articled to Edward Blore in 1844. He moved to the firm of Sir Matthew Digby Wyatt, one of the designers of the 1851 Great Exhibition, then in 1853 joined Henry Clutton, where he became a partner. He set up his own practice in 1856. The son of a civil engineer, Burges had a well-to-do background and was able to travel through Europe, studying architecture at first hand. Already inspired by gothic revivalists, such as A. W. N. Pugin, Burges conceived his early French Gothic style on his travels and fell under the influence of the scholarly Viollet-le-Duc.

Burges's first successful commission was the cathedral of St Finbar in Cork, begun in 1863. The following year he designed a chapel for Worcester College, Oxford, and in 1867 he began work at Knightshayes Court in Devon. In 1865 he met the 3rd Marquess of Bute, who shared his passion for medieval architecture and became his chief patron. When Bute came of age, in 1868, the pair began work on rebuilding Cardiff Castle. Castell Coch was started in 1872. The two projects occupied Burges right up until his death.

Llanfyllin: The Council House
A Georgian house of the 1740s that was home to captured French officers in the Napoleonic Wars. One room is decorated with grisaille murals painted by one of the prisoners.

Llangoed Hall
A Jacobean house of 1632, rebuilt in 1913 by Clough Williams-Ellis; he added a steep hipped roof with Arts-and-Crafts style dormers.

Llanrwst Almshouses
Charitable foundation created in 1610 to provide shelter for 12 deserving men of the village. The almshouses form a row along a lane, with an enclosed courtyard.

Llanvihangel Court
Tudor mansion of 1559, made symmetrical in the 1620s and restored in the 20th century to remove Edwardian additions.

Lloyd George's Boyhood Home
A simple two-up, two-down cottage where David Lloyd George grew up after his father died. The parlour was reserved for the children's lessons.

Machynlleth: Royal House
An Elizabethan town house with merchant's storeroom below. Reputedly Charles I spent the night here.

Maesmawr Hall
A black-and-white manor house on a cruciform plan, with a central chimneypiece serving all rooms. Damaged by fire in the 18th century, Maesmawr was restored in the 19th.

Manorbier Castle
The Norman castle where Gerald of Wales, 12th-century chronicler, was born. A range of buildings survive, including a hall and chapel.

Margam Castle
An 1830s house in neo-Elizabethan style with a massive tower. The Palladian-style orangery predates the house, being designed by Anthony Keck in the 1780s.

Nanteos Mansion
Georgian house of 1739 with later additions, including 17th-century-style baroque window pediments. The music room has Rococo decoration and a screen of painted columns.

Old Beaupre Castle
Remains of an Elizabethan mansion, attached to a surviving medieval manor house. The courtyard has an impressive Renaissance-style frontispiece, possibly imported from England.

Oxwich Castle
Built in the 1520s Oxwich was more mansion than fortress, with a traditional hall house in the south range and an east range rising four storeys in a building of some grandeur.

Pembroke Castle
The most important base of Norman power in south-west Wales. Rebuilt in 1204 by William Marshall, whose circular keep still dominates.

Pennal: Cefn Caer
Medieval farmhouse within a Roman camp, claimed as one of Glyndwr's homes. The new hall chimney, c1525, hid the original behind.

Penrhyn Castle
Begun in 1820 by Thomas Hopper in neo-Norman style, to replace an earlier gothick house by Wyatt. Norman motifs proliferate in the monumental interiors.

Picton Castle
A medieval castle with four towers and Great Hall, Picton was converted in the 18th century placing the main rooms on the first floor. A Regency castellated wing was added in 1800.

Plas Newydd (Llanfairpwll)
Medieval house rebuilt in gothick style in the 1780s and 90s to designs by Wyatt. Exterior gothick elements were removed in the 1930s; a Rex Whistler mural of 1939 is inside.

Plas Newydd (Llangollen)
Home of the 'Ladies of Llangollen', who in the late 18th century transformed a farm cottage with fabulous carved wood interiors.

Plas Teg
This early Jacobean mansion, with symmetrical façade and corner towers, survived unchanged through the 18th and 19th centuries and was saved by the present owner.

Plas yn Rhiw
A house of 17th-century origins in beautiful gardens and with a dramatic outlook. Restored in the 20th century, with additions to the interior by Clough Williams-Ellis.

Portmeirion
A village created by Clough Williams-Ellis, begun in 1926. Many of the houses were imported, rescued from destruction elsewhere, while new buildings show a range of styles.

Portmeirion: The Town Hall
Built by Clough Williams-Ellis as a community centre, the town hall is constructed around a 17th-century Great Hall, with a remarkable plasterwork ceiling rescued from Emral Hall.

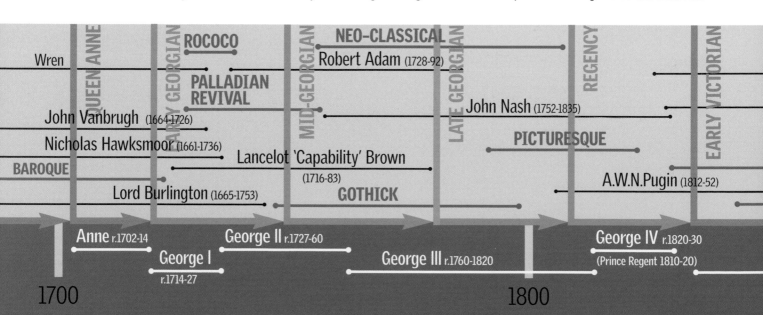

Powis Castle
The castle's red sandstone exterior dates from the 14th to 16th centuries. The grandest interiors were inserted during the Restoration by William Winde.

Presteigne: Judge's Lodgings
Courtroom and lodgings for visiting assize judges, rebuilt in 1826. The street façade is in classical Regency style, with central pediment.

Raglan Castle
Showpiece castle of the mid 15th century, converted into a Tudor palace in the 16th reflecting European Renaissance style.

Ruthin Castle
Designed by Master James of St George in the 1280s, slighted in the Civil War, then rescued in the 19th century when a house was built linked to the ruins.

Ruthin: Nantclwyd House
A timber-framed town house, dated to 1435, with rooms reconstructed to reflect various eras in the house's past.

St Davids: Bishop's House
A Norman palace rebuilt by the mid-14th-century Bishop Gower. The decoration that survives is evidence of former grandeur.

St Donat's Castle
A fortified manor, with encircling walls and gatehouses but no keep, restored in 1925 by W. R. Hearst with additions from other historic houses.

St Fagans
Museum of architecture in the grounds of St Fagans Castle, an Elizabethan house. The Rhyd-y-car cottages were originally at Merthyr.

Soughton Hall
House built in 1714 and altered by Charles Barry in the 1820s. In the 1860s the exterior was transformed with a new brick façade.

Tenby: Merchant's House
A 15th century town house with the shop and kitchen on the ground floor, living rooms on the first floor and bedrooms on the second.

Tower
A house of ancient origins, possibly a fortified farmhouse, with surviving medieval tower complete with residential rooms.

Clough Williams-Ellis 1883–1978

Bertram Clough Williams-Ellis was born in Northamptonshire in 1883. His father was Welsh and the family moved to Glasfryn when Clough was just four years old. As an architect, Williams-Ellis was mostly self taught; he worked for a firm of architects for just three months before setting up his own practice in 1905. Eventually, he built up a successful business, designing a wide range of projects both in Wales and England.

After a distinguished army career in the First World War, for which he was awarded the Military Cross, Williams-Ellis returned to architecture but also became involved in what would today be termed 'environmental issues'. He became part of the Garden City movement and chaired the development committee for one of the first new towns, Stevenage. He was also active in promoting the notion of a Green Belt around cities and was a founder member of the Council for the Protection of Rural Wales.

Williams-Ellis is best known for creating the village of Portmeirion (see page 158), the fulfillment of a long-held ambition. He had been looking for land on which to build a coastal or island settlement for several years; he even looked as far afield as New Zealand, before he bought the property at Aber Iâ that eventually became Portmeirion. Williams-Ellis was knighted in 1971 for services to architecture and the environment.

Treberfydd
A neo-Tudor mansion topped with gables and chimneys, designed by J. L. Pearson in 1848, with two towers – one forming the entrance – and mullioned windows.

Tredegar House
A Restoration mansion built around an earlier medieval house in Anglo-Dutch style. The Gilt Room is one of the finest interiors in Wales.

Treowen
A Jacobean house from 1627, formed of two ranges originally three storeys tall; the front range was reduced in the 18th century.

Tretower Court
A medieval complex of which the earliest structure, the keep, dates back to Norman times. The hall house is 14th century, extended in the middle of the 15th.

Trevor Hall
Red-brick mansion built around 1742. The house has a grand façade only one room deep, with a rear corridor linking the front-facing rooms. Mementos of a former record-producer owner abound.

Trewern Hall
A timbered manor house, dating back to the 1560s. It was extended in the Jacobean era when wings and a jettied upper storey were added to achieve a more symmetrical plan.

Ty Hyll
A simple country cottage, c1475 – the name means 'ugly house' in English – built from undressed stones by outlaw brothers.

Ty Mawr
A Tudor farmhouse in a lonely valley, rebuilt in the late-Elizabethan era when a fireplace and upper rooms were added. It has been restored to its 17th-century state by the National Trust.

Usk Castle
A castle of the de Clares, built in the 12th century; the Norman keep can still be seen. The castle was fortified with a garrison tower against Llywelyn the Great in the 13th century.

Weobley Castle
Started in the early 14th century and rebuilt in the late 15th, Weobley was converted into a mansion in the 16th century. The different eras are still evident in the castle's exterior.

Wern Isaf
An Arts-and-Crafts house designed by Herbert North in 1900. The unusual layout is based on a butterfly shape, with rooms opening out from the centre of the house like wings.

White Castle
A Norman fortress extended in the mid 13th century against attacks by Llywelyn the Less. The castle and inner ward are surrounded by a moat; the gatehouse has twin drum towers.

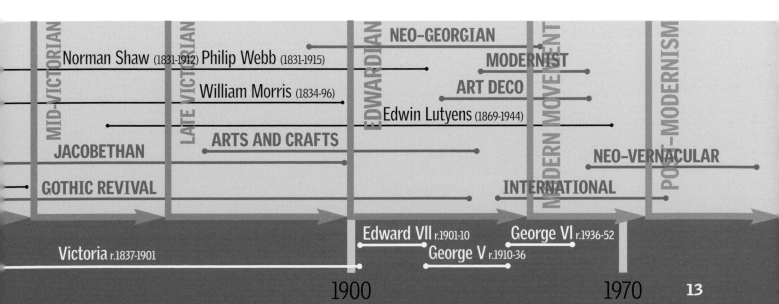

Clwyd

Chirk Castle

Clwyd

Bodelwyddan

★★★ Castellated mansion with portrait gallery and restored Arts and Crafts interiors

Near St Asaph, 17 miles NW of Mold; museum, open part year

Considering the troubled history of the north-Welsh Williams family over the centuries it is a miracle that anything survives at Bodelwyddan. Yet survive it does, nobly set on a rolling slope above the Vale of Clwyd, cocking a snook at an ugly hospital just below. The land passed from the ancient Humphrey (or Wmffre) family to Sir William Williams in the 1690s. The latter had been a controversial Speaker of the Commons under Charles II and his eldest son founded the Williams-Wynn dynasty, owner of extensive estates across north Wales.

An old house on the site went through various transformations, including a neo-classical remodelling in 1800-8. It was rebuilt in the 1830s in castellated gothic by Hansom and Welch. The estate remained heavily in debt until rescued by a Williams daughter, Lady Margaret Willoughby de Broke, who returned to Wales on her husband's death in 1852. She brought his money with her and earned from her in-laws the nickname, 'the Welsh robber'.

By the time of the Great War the house and estate were again 'embarrassed' and passed to the army. This experience was predictably unhappy, the neighbouring camp of Kinmel being the scene in 1919 of the Kinmel Mutiny against poor living conditions. The house later became Lowther College for Girls until it closed, again heavily indebted, in 1982.

Bodelwyddan was rescued by Clwyd County Council with a consortium of Warner low-cost hotels, saviour of a dozen English houses, and in collaboration with the National Portrait Gallery. The castle is now a mix of gallery, museum, hotel, park, shops and café, clinging dramatically to the hillside amid its formal gardens.

The Council's redecoration of the main rooms in the 1980s, under the direction of Roderick Gradidge of the Art Workers Guild, is a bravura work of Victorian revivalism. The rooms have been given furniture as well as paintings and thus seem

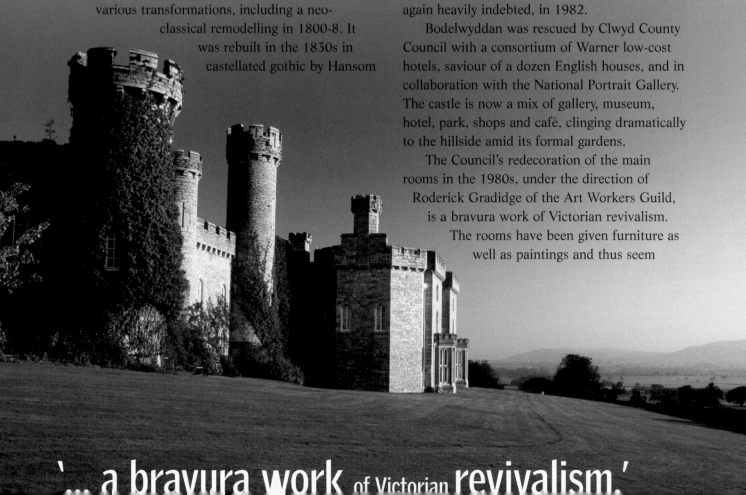

'... a bravura work of Victorian revivalism.'

Above Portraits by George Frederic Watts (1817–1904) line a corridor at Bodelwyddan. Watts was one of the most prominent artists of 19th-century Britain. In the 1850s he began painting his 'Hall of Fame' portraits of famous Victorians; included in the series were representations of Tennyson, Browning and Millais.

warmer and more lived-in than most museums. Given the loss of decorative plans of the old house, Gradidge had a free hand to recreate an Arts and Crafts interior and left his masterpiece.

Paintings inevitably dominate the interior. A corridor is devoted to portraits by G. F. Watts. The billiard room is lined with Spy cartoons. A fine portrait of Lady Dilke, 'art historian and feminist', hangs in the dining room. Most dramatic of all, the gothic drawing room has a Lawrence of Sophia Coutts. Signage and education are kept firmly in the background.

Bodrhyddan

⭐⭐ William and Mary mansion with Victorian additions by Nesfield

Near Rhuddlan, 16 miles NW of Mold; private house, open part year

Every Welsh county should have a Bodrhyddan, a mansion in the custodianship of the family that built it, cares for it and accepts its role in the community. Though open only infrequently in the summer, both house and garden are a monument to the Conwys, who arrived with Edward I as constables of his fortress at neighbouring Rhuddlan and have stayed ever since.

Visitors down the long drive are greeted by a theatrical Victorian frontispiece in Anglo-Dutch revival by Eden Nesfield. It was designed in 1872 when he was working on the more substantial Kinmel along the coast. The character of the house derives from the relationship of this façade to the two earlier houses on the site. One was Sir Richard Conwy's hall house of *c*1450, walling of which can be seen at the back, and the other a William and Mary building of 1696 which forms the central bays of the south front.

The Nesfield façade is a strongly vertical composition of three storeys with an attic just five bays wide. A pedimented front door rises to a balconied second storey on huge brackets, matching pilasters above and a dormer crowned by the family crest, a pelican. It might be a townhouse in The Hague. This feature is balanced by single-storey wings for a billiard room and conservatory on either side.

Moving to the south front (seen above), we see Nesfield neatly enclosing the five bays of the 17th-century house in a forest of mansards, dormers and chimneys, like a family portrait of relatives round ageing parents. In front is a parterre with stern yews designed by Nesfield's father, W. A. Nesfield, replacing what was the entrance drive to the earlier house.

The interior was substantially rearranged by Nesfield and is enjoyably crammed with family memorabilia and pictures. The entrance hall contains an armoury of weapons, with an Egyptian

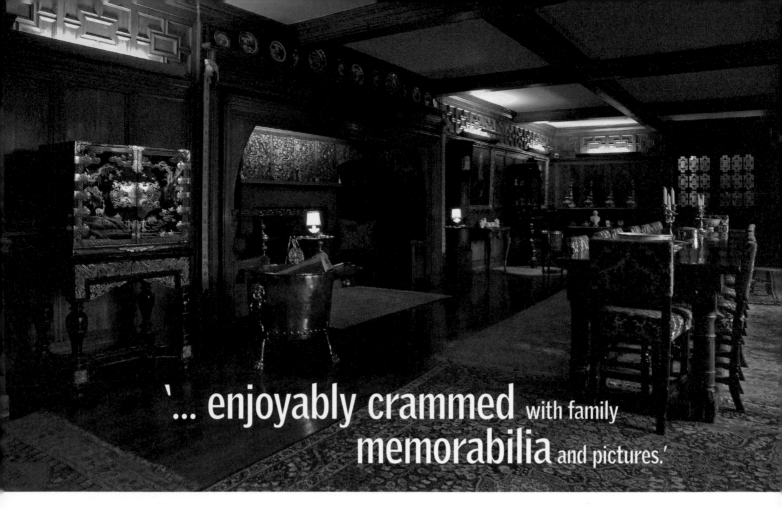

'... enjoyably crammed with family memorabilia and pictures.'

Above In the centre of the medieval Great Hall stands an ancient table which was left to Bodrhyddan by Marjorie, the last of the Shipleys of Twyford near Winchester. It is believed to have been used by the monks at Twyford when receiving tithes due to the monastery. Legend also has it that William II (Rufus) was taken to Twyford Abbey after he was shot and killed by an arrow while out hunting in the New Forest in August 1100; reputedly, the King's body was laid to rest for a night on this very table, before being taken to Winchester Cathedral for burial.

museum to one side. This contains a mummy collected by a Conwy on her honeymoon in 1836. Beyond is the old Great Hall, still so called, with a long medieval dining table and family portraits. Nesfield refashioned the old fireplace into an Art Nouveau inglcnook.

A staircase leads to the spacious drawing room, formed of the chamber over the hall and the wings of the William and Mary house incorporated as alcoves. The room is flooded with light, enhanced by the repainting in white and gold of two chimneypieces, probably imported by an antiquarian family member, William Shipley. He also revived the Conwy name which had been lost through female descent.

Shipley's chimneypieces, probably of Continental origin, are the most remarkable feature of the house. They were probably bought, like many church fittings, during a boom in the market in European antiques that followed Napoleon's depradations. They are in high baroque, displaying acanthus swirling and drooping round panels of biblical and other scenes. These panels were allegedly looted from an Armada ship wrecked off Anglesey, in which case they must have been inserted into later frames. A similar chimneypiece dominates the so-called Dean's dining room downstairs, but here in its original black, heavy and gloomy in consequence.

Bodrhyddan deserves to be better known. Its grounds, laid out by Nesfield and embellished by Clough Williams Ellis, include redwoods, a new summer house and an ancient well whose spring never dries. Its wellhead is attributed to Inigo Jones in 1612.

Above Chirk's magnificent gates were originally part of an ironwork screen on the north side of the castle; they were moved to their current position in 1888. **Right** The saloon is one of Chirk's fine neo-classical State Rooms; before 1772 it was used as the main dining room of the house. **Far right** The long gallery was created in the 1670s; the Rococo chimneypieces were 18th-century additions, while the ribbed ceiling was the 19th-century work of A. W. N. Pugin.

Chirk

★★☆ Marcher castle with Tudor and Georgian state rooms

Near Chirk, 7 miles S of Wrexham; National Trust, open part year

I first saw Chirk as the ancients would have seen it, looming out of the mist on a wild rainy day across the surrounding fields. It looked as implacable as once it was impregnable. The visitor must walk up from the car park, in bad weather fighting the elements and arriving at the great gate like a Welsh interloper assaulting a Marcher lord.

The castle was Roger Mortimer's contribution to Edward I's conquest of Wales, built between 1295 and 1310. Like most border castles it passed through many hands and lost many heads until the arrival of more settled Tudor times. It was bought by a successful Denbigh merchant, Thomas Myddelton, who went on to be a founder-member of the East India Company and Lord Mayor of London. His brother, Hugh, created London's water supply, the New River Company in Islington, where he is recalled in Myddelton Square.

Myddelton's son fortified Chirk for Parliament in the Civil War but saw it seized by local royalists. He was then forced to lay siege to his own house, which he was understandably reluctant to damage. Like many Welshmen, Myddelton became a royalist late in the day and was

eventually besieged by a Parliamentary force. He contrived to hold on until the Restoration, and remained secure in his ownership thereafter. Subsequent Myddeltons added to the Tudor state rooms round the courtyard with 18th and 19th-century insertions and alterations. The castle was rented in 1911 to Lord Howard de Walden, a medievalist eager for a proper castle. He staged jousts and falconry fairs in the grounds and filled the rooms with armour and weapons. On one such occasion a guest came down to breakfast to find his lordship reading *The Times* in full chain mail. It is said that when the Myddeltons resumed occupancy after the Second World War, the younger de Waldens were unaware that they did not own the place. Myddletons departed only recently.

The exterior is as built in the 14th century, with only the insertion of Tudor windows to suggest domesticity. The courtyard retains its medieval appearance; like Berkeley in Gloucestershire and Skipton in Yorkshire, it is one of few British castles that still does. The entrance is through the Cromwell Hall, a recreation by Pugin of what would have been Myddelton's Great Hall. It is appropriately rich in panelling, weaponry and heraldry. Coats of arms are of Myddeltons down the ages. On the screen hangs a picture of Chirk made of bog oak inlaid with bone.

The hall leads via a screens passage to the main staircase, a bold classical insertion of 1778 hacked out of the medieval walls. It appears to herald a suite of Georgian state rooms but does so only briefly. The state dining room is Adam in style by a Chester mason, Joseph Turner, and is laid

Right In 1645 Charles I spent two nights at Chirk and the King's Bedroom may, or may not, be the room in which he stayed. The canopied bed bears an inscription claiming that Charles slept in it, but the frame of the bed has been dated to *c*1700, half a century after the King was beheaded. It is also known to have come from a house in Essex, the childhood home of Elizabeth Rushout, who married Richard Myddleton in 1761.

out for dinner under the gaze of a boulle clock by Balthazar. The saloon has been plunged in National Trust gloom to protect its Mortlake tapestries, rendering Turner's ceiling and a set of school-of-Lely portraits near invisible. An exquisite Shudi harpsichord carries accomplished marquetry. On a wet day the whole room might be under water.

The small drawing room turns the corner to the long gallery, an earlier Restoration room with an oak floor big enough to make a good indoor cricket pitch. Here stands Chirk's glory, the ebony cabinet given by Charles II to Myddelton as a reward for turning royalist in the Civil War. It is beautifully inlaid, with ivory and tortoiseshell framing scenes from the life of Christ. The windows here offer views over the park to the surrounding countryside. The yew hedges in the formal garden are immaculate. Off the gallery is the King's Bedroom with a bed in which Charles I is improbably said to have slept. (Did he lie in a hundred such beds for distribution to faithful courtiers?) Across the courtyard the servants' hall is dark and austere, as if awaiting a Cromwellian sermon. On the wall hang portraits of castle servants. Adam's Tower is a survivor of a medieval residential tower, sadly denuded of furnishings.

Chirk's park gates are a delightful surprise. They are the masterpieces of the Welsh ironsmiths, the Davies brothers, designed in *c*1719. In a wild Welsh Rococo, they echo Tijou's gates at Hampton Court, a swirling tableau of foliage and birds round the Myddletons' wolf motif, forming an elegant welcome to a supposedly grim fortress.

Erddig

★★★★☆ Late 17th-century house with glorious Georgian interiors

2 miles S of Wrexham; National Trust, open part year

Erddig is the jewel in the crown of Welsh country houses. It may lack the punch of Powys (see page 175) or the fireworks of Cardiff Castle (page 78), but it has a depth of character, a sense of habitation blessed by age, of few houses in Britain. Erddig is impossible not to love. As restored by the National Trust, it evokes the lives of all who resided within its walls, rich and poor.

The opening line of the guide must apply to a hundred houses: 'In 1682 Joshua Edisbury was appointed High Sheriff of Denbighshire: it was to be the making of Erddig and the unmaking of Edisbury.' He set about building himself a mansion, by Thomas Webb of Cheshire, in the Restoration style of Roger Pratt. It had a basement and hipped roof and was furnished as well as money could buy. Within ten years Edisbury was hopelessly in debt. He turned for help to Elihu Yale,

later of New England, and to a wealthy brother, but to no avail. He died in London in disgrace and the house passed to Sir John Trevor, Master of the Rolls, and then in 1716 to another Chancery lawyer, John Mellor.

Mellor was a tight-fisted bachelor 'not very agreeable to the country', but he saved Erddig. He built wings to the original house and turned what had been the house of a local landowner into that of a London grandee, filling it with superb furnishings. In 1724 his steward wrote to him that since his last visit, 'There have been four coaches full of gentry...who admired the Hall and furniture mitily'. The house passed to Mellor's nephew, Simon Yorke, in whose family it remained to the end.

Of all the tales of the triumphs and woes of British country houses few equal that of the Yorkes of Erddig. Never grand or attaining high office and often desperately poor, they held to one principle, that their house and its contents were the genius of the place and must not be touched, let alone sold. At the end of the family's ownership in the 1960s, Philip Yorke could be found camping in his own freezing room, the walls subsiding into coal workings, rain pouring onto the state bed, wallpaper peeling and calor gas bills piling up. He struggled to make a living as a prep schoolmaster, security guard and tour operator with his own minibus. But nothing was touched. Erddig passed to the National Trust in 1973 virtually as it was in the 18th century.

Externally the main body of the house is undistinguished. The nine-bay east front to the garden lost its balance with the addition of wings, while its frontispiece is modest. The west front was

Far left The Little Parlour of 17th-century Erdigg was enlarged and adpated by Philip Yorke in 1775 to create the current library. **Left** Four years earlier, Yorke had enlarged the Saloon by joining two rooms into one; he retained the original 17th-century panelling. **Below** Yorke moved the State Bed to a new room on the first floor in 1770; prior to this, the Best Bedchamber had been on the ground floor. The original hand-painted Chinese wallpaper was removed in the 1970s for conservation treatment, before being reinstated in 1977.

refaced in 1772 and is dull. The excitement is inside. The main rooms are mostly 17th-century. Domestic offices fill the lower ground floor, giving the estate a sense of oneness with the family. Here are the agent's office, the housekeeper's room, the butler's pantry and the servants' hall, a single factory embracing domestic and estate management. The hall is hung with portraits of servants, a family tradition under the Yorkes and justly celebrated. They include the carpenter, woodman, butcher, 'housemaid and spider-brusher' and a black coach boy with a horn. Wandering these rooms makes it hard not to regard the family upstairs as tangential to the main enterprise.

The ground floor was altered by the Yorkes in the 18th century when the state bedroom was moved upstairs and replaced in 1827 by a neo-classical dining room designed by Thomas Hopper. It is filled with portraits of Yorkes and Custs (of Belton in Lincolnshire), the family into which the Yorkes married in 1770. The Saloon dates from the 17th-century house and looks out over the formal garden. It has rich panelling and excellent furniture, much of it dating from Mellor's acquisition. There is a boulle bureau veneered in brass and tortoiseshell. Mellor was fascinated by mirrors and collected superb pier-glasses.

The Tapestry Room is hung with Soho works, again commissioned by Mellor. In the centre is a Delft vase made for William and Mary and reputedly a gift from Queen Anne. The Chinese Room is filled with porcelain. The library contains a set of drawings illustrating 'the Royal Tribes of Wales' by Joseph Allen. The old entrance hall, now music room, has an enjoyable collection of 'after Lelys

and Knellers'. The private chapel was created by Mellor, the social gradations of the house replicated in the pew arrangements, with a classical reredos of 1663. The window glass includes fragments from the 15th century.

Upstairs at Erddig is now all bedrooms, cluttered with furniture and, in the case of the nursery, toys and a doll's house. The showpiece is the State Bedroom and its early 18th-century bed, hung with precious silks and with a counterpane of peacocks. The room displays an exquisite japanned bureau and laquered Chinese screen, surrounded by green Chinese wallpaper. Much was given to the family by Yale, then a governor in India.

The two ends of the bedroom floor are divided by a charming gallery running east-west. Apart from a collection of Dutch and other pictures it displays two models, one of the Chinese Pagoda at Kew and another of the Temple at Palmyra. The Blue Bedroom includes a set of mezzotints by Thomas Frye in an expressively mannerist style. The attic floor is filled with junk, temporary exhibitions and conservation in progress. Erddig is a house that never stays still.

The outbuildings survive intact, demonstrating the self-sufficiency (we would now call it sustainability) of a pre-20th century estate. We see joiner's shop, sawmill, wagon shed, blacksmith, stables, dairy, laundry, bakehouse and a kitchen with a large Venetian window. The habit of the Yorkes of composing doggerel about Erddig is everywhere on display. Hence a laundress 'though by duty of her post,/ She is less often seen than most,/ Her tuneful song in accents clear,/ Is heard within our Chapel here.'

The formal garden is a triumph of dignified conservation, never having been overwhelmed by Georgian picturesque or naturalism. The woods were home to a Victorian nightingale so celebrated that, reports the guide, 'half Wrexham would be in the wood until a late hour of the night…[and] several unpropitious matches as well as a considerable augmentation of the population, to be provided for from the parish rates, were the result of the amorous power of his soft lay.'

Greenfield: Pentre farmhouse

✶ Reconstructed Welsh longhouse, restored to its 17th-century state

Near Holywell, 9 miles N of Mold; museum, open part year

Wales is well-endowed with old farmhouses but few are accessible. Thanks are due therefore to country museums such as St Fagans in the south and the more modest Abbey Farm at Greenfield in the north. Part of the Greenfield Valley Heritage Park, it stands next to Norman Basingwerk Abbey, of which a few walls remain in a meadow down the road from Holywell. Adjacent to the abbey was an old farm and it is this that formed the basis of what is now a small museum.

Pentre farmhouse was moved to the museum in 1983 from the slopes of Moel Famau some six miles inland. It is a simple hall house dating from the 16th century but altered an estimated eight times since, of which the fourth (17th-century) was chosen for the rebuilding. This was when a byre and hall with dais was converted into a two-storey house with staircase tower and upstairs bedroom. The byre thus remains in place downstairs and the hall is supplemented by a parlour. This was the pattern of a typical Welsh longhouse. Windows have both stone and wood mullions.

The house is presented in the current 'country-life' style, with whitewash and flagstones and a pair of waxwork figures. The rooms are furnished to look contemporary with the rebuilding. Health and safety is not too intrusive, apart from a ludicrous burglar alarm on the wall (of a longhouse!).

A second, Victorian, farm Cwm Llydan, has been reconstructed near by, illustrating the improvements of a further two centuries of housing development. The improvements seem limited.

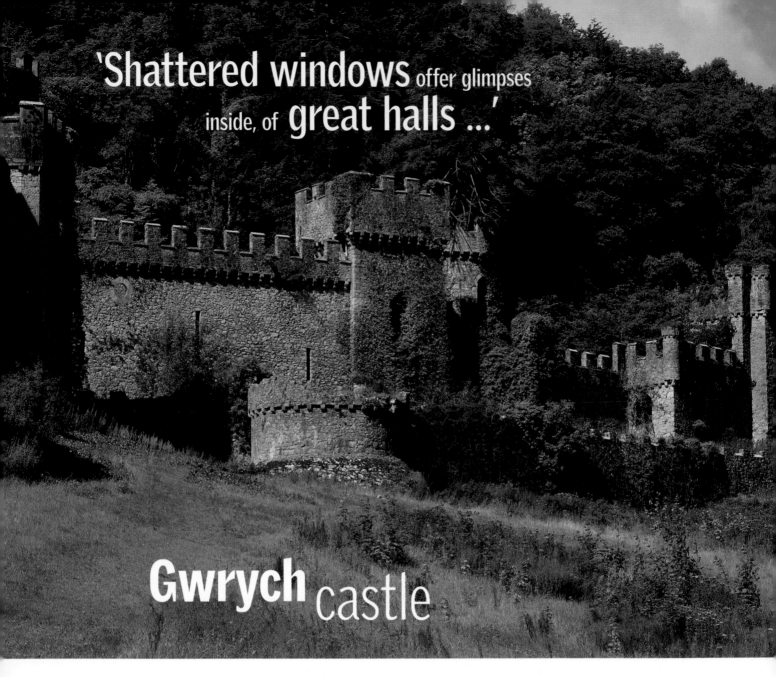

'Shattered windows offer glimpses inside, of great halls ...'

Gwrych castle

⭐⭐ Regency fantasy castle on a hillside, awaiting restoration

Near Abergele, 12 miles E of Conwy; private house, exterior only can be viewed

Even as a ruin Gwrych merits two stars. It ranks with Hafodunos Hall (see page 30) and Kinmel Park (page 33) among the saddest and most shocking ruins in Wales, all within a few miles of each other. Until the 1990s this was an intact Victorian castle/mansion clinging to the mountainside of Cefn yr Ogol, overlooking the Irish Sea towards Prestatyn. The Hesketh family, creators of Gwrych, famously compared this view to the Bay of Naples. When the sun shines and the towers of Liverpool can be seen in the far distance, the comparison is apt.

Gwrych (pronounced gritch) is the most remarkable relic, perhaps in all Britain, of the romantic gothic revival of the early-19th century, a nostalgia for medieval chivalry and valour and a conscious aversion to the industrial revolution. It was created on his wife's land by Lloyd Hesketh Bamford-Hesketh, whose family were among the richest of the ancestral grandees of Lancashire. On coming into his inheritance in 1816, Hesketh commissioned Charles Busby (co-planner of Regency Brighton)

28

to build what he, Hesketh, had sketched as a fantasy castle. In this he was helped by the gothic antiquarian, Thomas Rickman.

The structure was to be a Welsh Windsor, with state rooms and private apartments behind an astonishing façade of castellated towers, turrets, outhouses and conservatories. The irregular outline curved round the hillside with deliberate theatricality, producing reputedly the longest built façade in Britain. It was not completed until 1853, by when Rickman's gothic windows were made of cast iron.

The castle enjoyed barely a century of glory, chiefly under Hesketh's Welsh-speaking daughter Winifred, Countess of Dundonald, who died in 1924. Estranged from her husband, she left the house to sons whose interests lay in London and Scotland. It was used to house Jewish refugee children from Germany during the Second World War and was sold by the family in 1945, to endure a steady decline, first as a private house of the Salt family, then as a hotel (at which the boxer, Randolph Turpin trained), then a zoo, then private apartments and, in the 1980s, a bar and nightclub. In 1964 the park between the castle and the sea shore became a golf club. A succession of entrepreneurs bought the castle to use its land for caravans and chalets. By 1990 few could find out who owned the place and from 1994 onwards 'travellers' squatted the property and the interior was steadily destroyed by fires, apparently to the satisfaction of unknown American owners.

The disaster enveloping the house attracted the attention of an assiduous local teenager, Mark Baker, who sent letters to all and sundry, set up a website, wrote a book and formed a trust 'to preserve Gwrych'. He was phenomenally successful, even securing the attention of the Prince of Wales. At the time of writing, Gwrych had been acquired by Clayton Hotels, who seem determined to rebuild and restore it to its former glory.

Visitors can walk round the outside and admire the battlements rising high against the forest, and poke about in its extravagant outbuildings. Seen from below, from left to right, Gwrych comprises a garden temple, a melon and pineapple house, a French garden, the Conwy fly-tower, the outdoor theatre (of which there are two), the chapel and then the bulk of the main house. This is followed by the bothy, stables and brewhouse, a gigantic icehouse and a further lookout tower. To the rear can be seen the extensive service buildings of a Victorian mansion, including kennels cut into the hillside. Shattered windows offer glimpses inside, of great halls and stairways full of fallen rubble.

The thick forest, fast encroaching on the house, hides relics of the great days, including a miniature railway and a temple composed of a magic yew circle with a holm oak in its centre. From Gwrych's terraces the view east towards the Wirral can still evoke Italian fantasies, but increasingly not of Naples but of Pompeii.

Hafodunos hall

⭐ Victorian mansion by Gilbert Scott, now a roofless ruin

Near Llangernyw, 9 miles SE of Conwy; private house, exterior only can be viewed

Hafodunos is another Welsh tragedy. I include it only in the hope that, like Gwrych, it finds a saviour. Wales is rich in romantic valleys and lush settings for great houses, yet poor in surviving examples of the latter. Sir Gilbert Scott was an architect normally associated with churches and official buildings. He must have been exhilarated when asked by Henry Sandbach, son of a rich Liverpool trading family, to replace old Hafodunos on its steep hillside overlooking the River Gallen. While it does not rank with St Pancras or the Foreign Office, it certainly compares with his other great house at Kelham, in Nottinghamshire.

The house was begun in 1859 and decorated in collaboration with Margaret Sandbach's favourite sculptor, John Gibson, who supplied reliefs for the interior. The spectacular sloping grounds were laid out by Hooker. Like so many Victorian houses, Hafodunos enjoyed barely two generations of glory before a succession of deaths left the estate in the hands of a daughter, who sold it in 1934. It then endured a descent all too familiar with British houses in the mid-20th century, successively a girls' school, accountancy college, old people's home, hostel for the homeless and mental hospice. The building was closed as unfit in 1993 and plunged into the purgatory of awaiting planning permission for caravans and chalets. Its Grade I status, which in England is usually a spur to salvation, in Wales is so often an excuse for inaction and decay.

As dry and wet rot spread the house was steadily vandalized until, in 2004, two arsonists set it ablaze. Hafodunos is currently a gaunt, roofless ruin, Gibson's plaques staring out over collapsed stairs and gaping windows. Yet Scott's gables, chimneys and clock-tower stand. The polychrome walls and traceried windows still display mottos. The brick and stone are robust and those bold enough to trespass through the surrounding jungle can sense the spirit of the place. As for the grounds, thick with specimens brought back from Bhuttan and Sikkim, they remind me of Angkor Wat. At Hafodunos nature is seizing hold of the works of man.

'Hafodunos enjoyed barely two generations of glory ...'

Hartsheath estate

Near Pontbyddyn, 3½ miles SW of Mold; private houses, open by arrangement

Hartsheath Regency mansion with classical façade

This is a typically dignified mansion built for the new rich of the Regency. Its date is 1825 and its owner was the manager of a local mine, which appears not to have lasted long. The architect was a young man named Charles Mathews who, according to Hubbard in Pevsner, is 'better remembered as an actor', for which we must take his word.

The building might be a lesser work by John Nash, a classical box of five bays by five bays, of stone rather than Nash's brick and stucco and with an ascetic Doric porch. The last has been glazed to keep the draught from the hall. The internal arrangement is as expected, with a staircase rising four flights to a roof lantern, demonstrating how simply a fine staircase can transform a plain house into a grand one. The plasterwork throughout appears to be contemporary with the building, as are excellent marble chimneypieces.

The drawing room retains its Regency furniture, with wallpaper dating from 1841 according to graffiti in one corner. The house is furnished with portraits, watercolours and swords, in keeping with the style of the building. The current owner is an art historian and Oxford women's rugby blue. Hartsheath is in safe hands.

Fferm Late Elizabethan manor house

This miniature manor on the Hartsheath estate is apparently dated c1585 and not the emphatic 1506 over the porch. The house is of a conventional late-Elizabeth hall plan, with fireplace and chimney built in, not added later. One wing of the original H-plan has vanished, leaving just a hall with service wing rising two storeys to an attic. The interior is charming, a proper house occupied by tenants proud to show visitors round (by appointment). The tiny hall is divided from the entrance passage by its original screen with moulded uprights.

Flagstones cover the floor and heavy beams fill the ceilings, especially in the rear kitchen, which retains its fireplace and bread oven.

The staircase is appropriately cramped, lined with portraits of the Jones family of Hartsheath. Everywhere are sudden steps, beams and ancient cupboards. In one bedroom there appears to be an ancient oratory, if not priest's hole. The manor house is flanked by a medieval brew house and a courtyard of buildings of the same date, a delightful group.

Iscoyd park

⭐ ⭐ Georgian house of two parts with a grand library

2 miles W of Whitchurch; private house, open by arrangement

I warm to any house with a cricket field on its front lawn. Iscoyd, once the seat of the Godsal family with 2,000 acres, looks out across the flat country of Maelor Saesneg. This is the detached part of Flintshire east of the River Dee jutting into England and undeniably English in character.

The house is of three periods. The original was built *c*1700, but this was overwhelmed by a new formal block built towards the park in 1743, at right angles to the old one. This is of two storeys across five bays and faces the present drive. A front portico and dining room were added to this in 1843. Stern Georgian windows with white keystones knit the composition together, except at the back where a surviving Venetian window hints at something more dramatic.

The interior has the rooms of a busy family home. The exception is a Georgian-style print room composed entirely of pictures of dogs. What makes Iscoyd extraordinary is the wide rear staircase which links the later and earlier parts of the house. Decorated with a mural of the park, it leads to an architectural *coup de théâtre*, a library lying axially from front to back of the old building. It rises the equivalent of two storeys with a grand Rococo fireplace as its centrepiece, a breathtaking space.

Iscoyd retains a fine grouping of Stuart, Georgian and Victorian stables and farm buildings to the rear, including a delightful dovecote.

Kinmel park

★ Victorian mansion by Nesfield in Wren/Dutch renaissance style with Baroque stables

Near Abergele, 13 miles E of Conwy; private house, exterior viewed by arrangement

This is another house suspended between dereliction and hopeful restoration, currently viewable only outside. Kinmel is a major work of Eden Nesfield, a Loire chateau on the hillside overlooking the Vale of Clwyd. The estate belonged to the Hughes family, owners of the giant opencast Parys mine on Anglesey.

Successive houses on the site were either burned or demolished, until Hugh Robert Hughes visited Hampton Court with Nesfield in 1868 and calmly commissioned him to build something much the same. Hughes' initials (HRH) apparently gave him ambitions of royal grandeur. Kinmel is one of the earliest manifestations of the Queen Anne or 'Wrenaissance' revival, later brought to full realization by Nesfield's pupil, Richard Norman Shaw. It is thus important architecturally and historically and should never be demolished

The house emerges round a bend in a spectacular drive uphill across an open park. Woods loom above, accompanied by earlier stables in a neo-baroque style by William Burn, splendid enough to be a mansion in their own right. The effect is supremely theatrical, enhanced by an open gravel forecourt big enough to troop the colour. The gates, also by Nesfield, recall Tijou's at Hampton Court.

The main façade is a balanced, symmetrical composition of 19 bays. The central pavilion breaks the rhythm in architectural syncopation, narrowing the fenestration and thrusting the eye upwards to a steep roof with dormers and a lofty chimney. The effect is similar to that created by Norman Shaw at Bryanston in Dorset. The walls are of red brick with pilasters and stone dressings, the windows and dormers white with close glazing bars.

The unrestored interiors include a two-storey ballroom and a 60-foot library and drawing room. After serving as an army billet during the war the house became a girls' school, Clarendon, and later a hotel/bar. A fire gutted the upper floor in 1975, also destroying the chapel.

On the main A55 is Nesfield's entrance lodge, the Golden Lodge, an exquisite work encrusted with Arts and Crafts motifs and renaissance detail. It is a major work of architecture, finer even than Nesfield's similar essays in this style at Kew.

Plas Newydd

At Llangollen, 9 miles SW of Wrexham; museum, open part year

Sarah Ponsonby and Eleanor Butler were of Irish parentage. They met in Kilkenny in 1768, when Sarah was 13 and Eleanor 29, and fell in love, or whatever that means to a 13-year-old. Despite desperate efforts by their parents, which had one sent to a convent and the other into marriage, ten years later they ran away together, only to be intercepted at Waterford dressed as men. Sarah was armed with a pistol and swore 'to live and die with Miss Butler'. Later that year the families capitulated and the ladies went to Wales where they found Llangollen 'the beautifullest country in the world'. In 1780 they resolved to live there 'a life of sweet and delicious retirement', which they did for 50 years. Unlike male homosexuals, who were imprisoned, they were regarded as eccentric, even admirable in their selfless devotion to each other.

The Ladies of Llangollen, as they became known, were widely celebrated for their lively company. Living on the route through Wales to Snowdonia, Holyhead and Dublin, a visit to 'the ladies' at Plas Newydd became a feature of early Welsh tourism, assisted by their gift for letter-writing and their accumulation of passing gossip. They corresponded with Byron, Canning, Burke

Right The Ladies of Llangollen made many changes to Pen-y-Maes, the cottage that became Plas Newydd. They set about making a range of decorative alterations, including the addition of an eclectic collection of wood carvings. The Ladies were not, however, responsible for the black-and-white timbering outside; this was added by General John Yorke, a later owner.

'It is a
place of delight
and a monument
to love.'

Above left The Ladies of Llangollen in a portrait on display in the house. The pair were well known for their eccentricities, which included a sober, masculine dress code. **Above right** The carved wood figures and panelling that adorn Plas Newydd came from a variety of sources, ranging from church furnishings to bedsteads.

and Castlereagh, and were visited by the Duke of Wellington, the Duke of Gloucester, Wordsworth, Scott, Sheridan and Wedgwood. Wordsworth wrote of 'Sisters in love, a love allowed to climb/ Even on this earth, above the reach of time!'

The ladies seldom left Llangollen. They dressed like parsons, their hair swept back and powdered, with top hat, cravat, petticoats and black coat. Eleanor wore various noble orders round her neck, giving her the look of an elder statesman. Their servant, Mary Carryl, came from Ireland and had a famous temper, which the ladies loved. The household emerges from many accounts as erudite – the library contained thousands of books – yet humorous, mischievous and extrovert, an engaging cul-de-sac of the English enlightenment.

The house had originally been a farm cottage. The ladies extended it and added the gothick oriel windows and porches, but it was a later owner who gave the exterior its present black-and-white appearance, composed of ornamental battens. The porch, including pieces donated by the Duke of Wellington, is as rich in decoration as an Italian baptistery. The house, seen across a lush lawn and with the surrounding hills as backdrop, is most picturesque.

The interior is almost beyond description. The rooms have been much altered but remain true to the spirit of the ladies' occupation. Their particular love was wood carving, and visitors were expected always to bring some item of wood to decorate the house. Hence every inch is encrusted with works from all over Europe, gothic and renaissance, religious and secular, together with ancient books and medieval glass fragments.

Upstairs is a 'state bedchamber' or spare bedroom, opposite the ladies' own bedroom. Downstairs are the oak room, hung with gilded leather, the dining room and the library. As at A La Ronde in Devon, also created by two ladies, the atmosphere is of Georgian curiosity, displaying the thrill of discovering new things and before the onset of Victorian heaviness.

Plas Newydd was acquired in 1876 by General John Yorke of Erddig (see page 23). He had known the ladies in his youth and turned the house into a museum in their honour, thus saving it for posterity. It was bought by the council in 1932 and has been well-restored, given that it was sold and cleared many times after Sarah's death in 1831. It is a place of delight and a monument to love.

Plas Teg

★★☆ Restored Jacobean masterpiece, refurnished with flair

At Pontbyddyn, 3 miles SW of Mold; private house, open part year

Plas Teg, ancestral seat of the Trevor family, is the most enjoyable early Jacobean house in Wales. This is largely due to its recent rescue by Cornelia Bayley. The house might easily have gone the way of Hafodunos (see page 30) and Gwrych (page 28), given the disregard of Flintshire council (now Clwyd) for its historic buildings. Instead it is eccentric and safe.

Plas Teg was built *c*1610 and shares an English renaissance plan with such contemporaries as Hardwick Hall, in Derbyshire, and Charlton House, in London. It was built for Sir John Trevor, an Elizabethan courtier/adventurer who became navy secretary under James I in 1611. Accused of fraud, he withdrew to his Welsh estate and erected a house in the style of an English grandee. Later Trevors and Trevor-Ropers recovered their fortunes and acquired Glynde Place in East Sussex. Plas Teg was never a principal residence and was thus never rebuilt in the 18th or 19th centuries.

The house was requisitioned in the war and eventually sold in 1944, to find its fate as a furniture store. In 1957 the owner applied for demolition, at a time when such houses were vanishing at the rate of one a month. This stung a reasonably prosperous member of the Trevor family, Patrick Trevor-Roper,

to step forward and buy the house, stabilizing it and passing it on to two historic building enthusiasts. They were defeated by the cost of its upkeep, and it was regularly vandalized and burgled.

The house reverted to dereliction until the arrival, in 1986, of Mrs Bayley, an indomitable antique dealer. Her first night was spent on the floor of the only room then watertight. She brought with her an obsession with the place, some money and a large number of parrots. She has turned it into a haunt of ghosts, paranormal investigators, artists and enthusiasts. It stands grey and forbidding, overlooking the Mold-Wrexham road, but the inside is a riot. Bayley's patronage of China's new trade in reproduction Western art accords (if only just) with the Jacobean flamboyance of the place.

The house façade is symmetrical, for four corner towers flanking three recessed and gabled bays. The design is complex, suggesting a plan by Robert Smythson. The hall runs front to back, with a great chamber directly above it on what is the principal floor. Bayley restored the hall, which was previously divided, and gave it flagstones, a fireplace and copies of works by Veronese and Rubens.

The ground floor has recovered its dining room (hung with 'Lelys') and parlour/drawing room, with French Empire furniture. Behind various curtains are concealed the kitchens and basements, crammed with Bayley's scouring of antique and car-boot sales the length and breadth of the nation. One room devoted entirely to parrots appears to be eaten by them.

Above left The chandelier in the drawing room was pieced together from damaged chandeliers by Plas Teg's current owner and restorer, Cornelia Bayley; she has created many similar light fittings throughout the house.
Above centre The timber and plaster ceiling over the landing has survived from the 17th-century house, as has the staircase itself, which was reputedly made from timber salvaged from the Spanish Armada. When Cornelia Bayley bought Plas Teg, the woodwork of the stairs was covered in a layer of black paint.
Above right Each of Plas Teg's four corner towers has a bathroom on the second floor; the yellow bathroom is equipped with a tall Victorian shower.

The staircase has robust Jacobean balusters with, on the landing, a painted cloth in place of a tapestry. The great chamber has been restored with hand-stitched silk wall hangings. Most remarkable for a house of this size, every bedroom even on the second floor has been refurnished, with four-poster beds, paintings and sculptures. Bathrooms contain Bayley's collection of early plumbing. Some baths look like instruments of torture – one has a brazier underneath to heat its water. Every corner of Plas Teg is occupied by busts, faded prints, fans, rocking chairs, ornamental candles, artificial flowers, seashells and ghosts. It is a house resuscitated, joyfully celebrated by Mark Baker in his admirable history of the place.

Ruthin castle

★★ Medieval castle, transformed into a home in the 19th century

Castle Street, Ruthin; now a hotel

Ruthin is the most charming small town in Wales. I would pit it against England's Rye, Broadway or Lavenham. Every prospect pleases. Seventeenth-century and earlier private houses survive and the central square has the informal elegance of Ludlow. To crown everything, the Castle is not another Denbigh or Rhuddlan, a benighted mound of stone like so many handed down by the old Ministry of Works. The Victorians were ahead of the game and transformed the empty ruin. It is now a thriving hotel and the town is all the better for it.

Ruthin was awarded by Edward I to Reginald de Grey, Baron of Wilton, in 1282 as reward for help in his Welsh campaigns. Its location where the Vale of Clwyd is at its most lovely must have contrasted with the Anglo-Norman image of Wales as a place of savage

wilderness. None the less, Grey had to defend his holding against insurgency. Walls, a bridge, a chapel dedicated to St Peter and a castle were built to protect the small community of English colonists. The castle was designed by the architect of the age, Master James of St George.

A century later it was a feud between de Grey and Glyndwr that sparked the latter's rebellion. The town was sacked in 1400, de Grey being captured by Glyndwr and held to ransom, the payment of which ruined the family and helped finance Glyndwr's revolt. None the less the de Greys remained at Ruthin until 1508 when the castle was sold to the monarch and, in 1632, to the Myddeltons of Chirk. It was fortified for the king in the Civil War, thereafter being slighted and supplying stone to rebuild the town. It was a Myddelton, Maria West, who in 1826 decided to rebuild the castle as a house, linked by a picturesque bridge to the old ruin.

In 1849 his structure was extended by Maria's son to plans by Henry Clutton, in vivid red sandstone. Regency restraint became Victorian ostentation. The earlier white limestone was given red dressings. A long wall was built round the site with a neo-Perpendicular gate to the town. Wings, towers, graceful oriels and chimneys dart off everywhere. Magnificent trees decorate the grounds. It is a successful work of picturesque, with fragments of the old castle looming out of the vegetation or incorporated into the structure. Two large dragons flank the entrance.

The interior has been much abused since the house was sold in 1920 to become a clinic and in 1963 a hotel. It needs the flair of a Bodelwyddan. Yet some of the old swagger remains. There are antlers in the entrance hall, and the Grand Salon has a carved wooden fireplace displayed at the Great Exhibition.

Nantclwyd house

★★ Ancient town house restored to show seven periods of occupation

Castle Street, Ruthin; museum, open part year

In a side street off Ruthin's main square is a timber-frame house which recent tree-ring dating puts at 1435, though guidebooks plead the case for a 1314 original on the site. It was owned or built by a local weaver, Gronw ap Madoc, and later used as a girls' school, an Edwardian rectory and the judge's lodging for the town. It was in private hands until the 1980s and was eventually bought by the county council.

The value of the house today is in reflecting the traces of these various uses over the centuries. Rather than restore it to what would have been an ersatz medieval interior, the council have reinstated different rooms to demonstrate its appearance successively in 1435, 1620, 1690, 1740, 1891, 1916 and 1942. This is a remarkable museological feat.

The house exterior is black-and-white timbered with two prominent gable wings jettied forward to the road. The interior is inevitably an oddity, given the intention to reflect its 'pasts'. The hall is decorated for 1942 and the rector's study for 1916, with mild touches of Art Deco. The schoolroom is claimed for 1891 and the well-panelled Georgian bedroom for 1740, hung with Chinese wallpaper. A Jacobean 1620s room has yellow and purple painted fabrics and looks as if brand new (which once it was). The 1690s room, or 'cabinet', is brightly painted and decorated with Kidderminster-stuff hangings. After this the medieval chamber is almost an anticlimax.

Soughton hall

★★ Georgian mansion, adapted by Charles Barry and then John Douglas

Near Soughton, 2 miles N of Mold; now a hotel

Soughton Hall is one of the oddest houses in north Wales. From a distance down the magnificent lime drive it might be the product of a Victorian nightmare. On closer view it looks more friendly, perhaps a French railway terminus. This façade was designed in 1867 by the architect, John Douglas, and is now a hotel.

The house was built in about 1714 and acquired in 1732 by the bishop of Bath and Wells, formerly of St Asaph. His daughter married a Bankes, of Kingston Lacy in Dorset, and the house has been in the family ever since. The present structure was mostly built by a later William Bankes, antiquarian, roué and creator of the present Kingston Lacy. When he came into ownership of Soughton in the 1820s he had his architect, Charles Barry, give it a new splendour, but in 1841 Bankes had to flee prosecution for homosexuality and never returned to Britain.

Bankes's house was again altered in the 1860s by his nephew with the aid of Douglas, destroying whatever Georgian effect the exterior might have retained. Much red stone and brick were added. Windows were altered, the porch was made heavier and a cupola was replaced by a spiky turret.

The inside is still full of ghosts of various stages in the house's history. These include fittings, doors and fireplaces of the early 18th and early 19th-century alterations. The downstairs hall is clearly Georgian. There is a superb staircase sweeping up to a suite of state rooms, including saloon and dining room. The former has a Tudor-style beamed and stencilled ceiling, the latter a ceiling which Hubbard in Pevsner describes as 'looking like a progeny of the Brighton Pavilion'.

Tower

⭐ Remains of a medieval fortified farm with later additions

At Nercwys, 1 mile S of Mold; private house offering bed and breakfast, viewing by arrangement

Tower is hard to find on the southern outskirts of Mold. It has been in the same family for some 500 years and Charles Wynne-Eyton has restored it, tends its garden and invites all-comers to see and even stay (on selected days).

The house needs a detective rather than a historian. It appears to be a rare survival of a fortified farm on the Welsh side of the border. An original hall house has all but disappeared under later gentrification, but a late-medieval residential tower survives, with semi-circular stair turret. Records show it as built by the splendidly named Rheinallt Gruffydd ap Bleddyn in the 14th century. Legend has the English mayor of Chester hanged in its vaulted chamber in 1465.

This chamber forms the present dining hall, while the old hall above it has been divided into two grand bedrooms. Their windows, seen from outside, are remarkable. They must be 16th-century since for most of its subsequent life the house was a farm. No less odd are the magnificent gargoyles which crown the tower, beneath what is clearly a late-Georgian parapet. The interior panelling and furnishings are Victorian.

The house is very much inhabited, full of family paraphernalia. There are county maps, fans, old swords and an impressive breastplate with two bullet holes in it. Visiting doctors argue over which would have caused death. Though the house is modest, the gates to the road are worthy of a Chatsworth. They came from the grounds of a neighbouring Eyton property, Leeswood, and may be by the Davies brothers, whose finest work is at Chirk (see page 20).

Trevor hall

★★ Georgian mansion, saved from destruction and now restored

Near Llangollen, 8 miles SW of Wrexham; private house, open part year

The warm redbrick mansion is well sited overlooking the Dee, the Shropshire Union Canal and the A5, as they make their joint assault on Llangollen. It was a scat of the prolific Trevors and was owned by their descendants until the Second World War. The house was rented to the Edwards family in the 19th century and sold in 1956 to a local timber merchant who was allowed to fell the trees and applied for permission to demolish the house. This was refused in 1961 but the house survived just two years before being gutted by fire, an all-too-familiar Welsh occurrence. A farmer then roofed it for his cattle.

This ruin was acquired by a historic buildings enthusiast and saviour of many Welsh houses, Michael Tree, in 1987. He demolished the Victorian accretions, restored 73 sash windows and sold it to a record producer, Louis Parker, in the 1990s. Since Parker's death it has been decorated

Top A baby grand piano has pride of place in the music room on the first floor. **Above** The staircase is one of the few original features to have survived the fire at Trevor Hall in the 1960s. The music theme continues here, with a juke box once owned by record producer Louis Parker. Family photos line the staircase wall.

and opened for weekend hire by his widow, Louise. The furnishings are themed, wild, eccentric, kitsch and fun. Trevor is a mix of Plas Teg and pop art.

The house appears to be based on an early hall house, with lateral fireplace, off-centre entrance and side wings. This was rebuilt *c*1742 with a grand façade nine bays wide and a pedimented doorcase up a flight of stairs. These generous proportions are deceptive since the house is just one room deep with a corridor at the back, enabling all rooms to enjoy the view.

Tree carefully restored the interior to its Georgian proportions, including a central hall with large classical fireplace and staircase rising the full height of the house. The decoration is idiosyncratic. It embraces numerous mementos of rock groups promoted by Parker and should one day form a major collection of 1960s and 70s memorabilia. For the present a great house has come back to life.

Dyfed

Carreg Cennen Castle

Dyfed

Aberystwyth: The Old College

✶ ✶ Victorian fantasy hotel by the sea, converted into a university

King Street, Aberystwyth; private house, open by arrangement

Aberystwyth has long been a lost soul among Welsh resorts. Today, with a booming university community and a reviving leisure industry it is acquiring a new personality. It is appropriate that its most distinguished building is a hotel turned college dominating the sea front next to the ruins of the old castle. The site was that of a house built by John Nash (his first) for Uvedale Price as part of a project to turn Aberystwyth into a Regency resort, a Welsh Brighton. The hotel was intended to take this ambition forward into the railway age and in 1864 a design was commissioned from the neo-gothic architect, J. P. Seddon.

Within a year the hotel was bankrupt and the building was bought for £10,000 by a committee to found a national university of Wales (first mooted by Glyndwr). There followed three decades of arguing about money, with Seddon struggling to convert his hotel into a university and always on the brink of dismissal. The hotel had been intended to rank with Scott's at St Pancras and Broderick's at Scarborough but was sadly curtailed. Enough remains to render 'the Old College' one of the great Victorian buildings of Wales.

Seddon's original design is confined to the central block, entered on the landward side by an eccentric triangular *porte-cochère*. Both front and rear façades look a cross between a Welsh castle and a French chateau, billowing with towers, battlements, arcades and windows of every shape and style. The nine-storey towers echo the castle next door. Built of soft Bath stone the effect is never grim and every feature diverts the eye. A wooden gallery above the entrance conceals the

'... one of the **great Victorian buildings** of Wales.'

old roof-top gym. The exterior is coated in gargoyles and statue niches.

The two extensions to the south are clearly afterthoughts. The farthest is a science block, to whose tower Seddon added a mosaic mural by Voysey depicting a puzzled Archimedes being offered a steam engine and a sailing ship. Seddon had to remove a downcast pope, embodying superstition as the enemy of reason, from his design. The landward door to the science block is flanked by two warning serpents, one marked error and the other darkness. Aberystwyth clearly felt itself at the frontier of education.

The interior is now scruffily academic but includes a gothic stone staircase and a central hall. The latter is a curious chamber, Anglo-Indian in character, with a heavily corbelled gallery and timber roof. It is dominated by two larger-than-life statues of Welsh worthies, surely intended for a large public space.

Above The main entrance to the Old College is through an unusual triangular *porte-cochère*, located on the side of the building and facing away from the sea. **Below** On the southernmost tip of the building is a tower, with three mosaic panels by Charles Voysey created in 1887–8; the central figure is Archimedes as a representation of pure learning.

★ ★ ☆   Ruin of the greatest Welsh prodigy house

6 miles NW of Tenby; private house, open all year

More than any other house in Wales, Carew embodies the power of the Marcher lords and the splendour of their successors under the Tudor ascendancy. It was probably begun as a castle by Gerald of Windsor, first constable of Pembroke, under the authority of the Montgomerys, lords of the central March.

The rampaging campaign of Roger of Montgomery and his sons across mid-Wales under the authority of William II reached the site in 1093. They later overwhelmed the last independent king of Wales, Rhys of Deheubarth, who had been respected as such by William the Conqueror. In the process they captured Rhys's daughter, Nest. She became mistress of the future Henry I and was married to Gerald of Windsor as governor of Pembroke (see Cilgerran, page 53). The first Carew is reputed to have been built by him *c*1100 for her and her family, of which an old tower survives.

Most of Carew was begun two centuries later by Edward I's courtier, Sir Nicholas de Carew. He raised the two mighty drum towers that look out over the river and millpond,

Carew castle

Above The vaulted kitchen is in the eastern range of Carew Castle, built by Sir Nicholas de Carew between c1280 and c1310. The cooking would have been done over an open fire in the large fireplace. The room next door was the private room of the castle's steward, the servant in charge of the household.

with battered bases and tiny windows. This castle passed to the south Welsh grandee, Sir Rhys ap Thomas, whose troops lent crucial support to Henry Tudor at Bosworth.

Briefly the most prominent man in Wales, Rhys adapted Carew as his principal seat (with Weobley as a lesser one). In 1507 he celebrated his elevation to the Garter with a tournament of unprecedented lavishness. Six hundred nobles were treated to hunting, feasting, jousting and, as if in atonement, a penitential ride to St Davids. The event was regarded as the most lavish climax to the medieval era in Wales.

Under Henry VIII, Rhys's grandson went the way of many an Icarus and lost his head. Carew passed to the Crown and later to the Elizabethan courtier and probably illegitimate son of Henry VIII, Sir John Perrot. Rich from office in Ireland, Perrot converted Carew (and Laugharne) into a grand 'prodigy' house before also falling foul of the tyrannical monarch and ending his life in the Tower of London.

It is this structure that makes such a vivid impression today, albeit as a ruin. It is approached from the car park across an outer ward, presumably the site of Rhys's jousting,

and entered through an inner gatehouse next to the remains of the old Norman tower.

The inner ward is instantly impressive. The ruin of Rhys's Great Hall runs along the south range of the ward, its porch adorned with the arms of Prince Arthur, eldest son of Henry VII, and his then wife, Catherine of Aragon. This memorial to a brief union shines from the rough stone like a renaissance jewel.

The two earlier round towers at either end of the hall range were converted by Rhys as apartments, one of them supposedly to receive the king. But it is Perrot's grander house to the right of the ward that dominates the interior, the range facing over the water. This is plainly post-medieval, three storey's high and with tall Elizabethan windows and a long gallery above.

This is was among the greatest 16th-century buildings in Wales, still largely intact in Buck's engraving of 1740. Its appearance today, with walls rising their full height but floorless and roofless, is both sensational and tragic. This was Wales's Hampton Court and merits a more vigorous reinstatement than as a 'stabilized ruin'. If only Cardiff's Marquess of Bute had been a Pembrokeshire man.

Carreg Cennen castle

 ★ ★ Romantic citadel with a secret cave

Near Trapp, 4 miles SE of Llandeilo; Cadw, open all year

This is a castle of Arthurian fantasy. It commands a 300-foot rock thrust upwards from the basin of the Tywi valley like an Albigensian fortress. Whether floating on a mist in the early morning, or blazing at dusk in a moist Welsh sunlight, it seems unreal.

The site has yielded Roman remains. A fortress here was captured by the Normans and changed hands under the Llywelyns until rebuilt for the Crown in the late-13th century. It held out for a year against Glyndwr and was later garrisoned to deny it 'to brigands and robbers' (or Lancastrians) until demolished by the Yorkists in 1462.

By the 18th century Carreg Cennen had been transformed from menace to magnet. Well established in the picturesque canon, it was visited by Turner and later restored by the Earl of Cawdor, who sadly did not go further in his work than to 'create a ruin'. The view of the south front from below the cliffs is spectacular, as is the long walk up an ancient pathway from the road.

The castle proper is entered through an outer ward, now demolished, by means of a stepped ramp into the gatehouse. This ramp is overlooked by the entire north range of the castle and must have been impassable as a means of assault. The two northern towers, one round and the other with squared corners, still stand to half their height, as does the gatehouse. The inner ward retains the outlines of the great hall and chapel adjacent to it. The solar and some fireplaces and windows form part of Cawdor's part-restoration.

Most intriguing are the remains of a sally port at the south-east corner of the site, leading through a cave to the cliff below. This is accessible but finishes in a wall. Like all sally ports, it risked being as useful to an attacker as to a defender.

Cilgerran

✩ ✩ Ruin of an historic castle, high on a crag above a ravine

14 miles NE of Fishguard; Cadw, open all year

The valley of the Teifi is the most quietly beautiful in south Wales. Since the middle ages its fertile meadows made it rich in livestock. By the early 19th century, there were said to be over 40 gentry houses in the 20 miles below Llandysul. The valley's hunt claims to be among the oldest in Britain and refused to stand down even on the day of Queen Victoria's funeral.

Nowhere is Teifi's beauty more spectacular than from Cilgerran crag, a prominence worthy of the Dordogne. The castle is believed to have been built, like Carew (see page 50), by Gerald of Windsor to protect his northern flank against the Welsh pressing down from Powys – his fort called Cenarth Bychan is assumed to be Cilgerran. It was here in 1109 that Nest's celebrated abduction by Owain ap Cadwgan supposedly occurred, earning her the title of 'Helen of Wales'.

Nest was daughter of Rhys, last king of Deheubarth. Captured by the Normans in 1093 she became mistress of the future Henry I and bore him a son, FitzHenry. Granted to Gerald as wife in the hope of placating the Welsh, Nest came to Pembroke and bore four more children. Her reputation was such that men pined for a sight of her beauty. In 1109 her distant cousins, the Cadwgans, were raiding south from Cardigan in the neighbourhood of Cilgerran. The hot-blooded young prince, Owain ap Cadwgan, assaulted the castle with his friends, set fire to part of it and surrounded Nest and Gerald in their chamber. Nest pleaded with her husband to flee for his life down the latrine shoot. She and her children were carried off into the wilds of Cardiganshire. History has long debated her complicity in the venture.

No Norman was likely to accept such humiliation, let alone from the Welsh, and the outcome was predictably bloody. Nest managed to return to Carew, and years later Owain was tracked down and killed by Gerald's Flemish archers. After Gerald's death Nest married twice again, to Normans, her career symbolizing the unstable fusion of conqueror and conquered over the century after the conquest. Today's visitors look in vain for the latrine shoot, but there could be no more romantic venue for Nest's story.

The castle was rebuilt by William Marshall (see Pembroke Castle, page 68) after the Llywelyn uprising with two of his characteristic drum towers overlooking the entrance. With a precipice guarding the far wall they must have made Cilgerran near impregnable. It withstood an assault by Glyndwr but soon fell into ruin. Today the view down into the woody gorge is as awesome as ever. On the river below that peculiarly Welsh craft, the coracle, is still in use.

Cresselly

The Georgian house, that sits at the end of an impressive drive, was built in 1769 by a local architect, William Thomas of Pembroke, in the Adam style. The client was a local landowner, John Allen. Its five-bay villa façade would have been beautifully proportioned before the addition of Victorian wings, whose bays clumsily seek to mimic the central block.

The garden front remains handsome under a low hipped roof. The interior, shown to visitors by a descendant of the original owners, Hugh Harrison-Allen, is that of a comfortable gentry house. Rooms are furnished in period taste and walls hung with family portraits, the ladies in the style of their period, the men in soldiering or hunting uniform that has remained constant over centuries.

The house contains an exceptional library with built-in Regency bookcases. But the jewel is the ceiling of the drawing room, a swirling, vigorous Rococo composition with tendrils radiating from the centre as if about to trail down the walls and envelop the room. The craftsmen were believed to be Italians from the Bristol area. It is a delight to find such a masterpiece hidden away in a Welsh country house.

Left A 1982 bust of Hugh Harrison-Allen stands on an 18th-century oak coffer in the staircase hall, while portraits of his great-uncles hang on the walls; the 1st Earl of Hertford, a distant relation, looks down from above.

Dinefwr: **Newton** house

★★☆ Restoration mansion with Victorian exterior, set in a deer park

1 mile E of Llandeilo; National Trust, open part year

Dinefwr was the seat of the kings of Deheubarth and as such was capital of Celtic south-west Wales. It was here that King Rhys's daughter, Princess Nest, would have been born and from here that he set out to his death at the hands of the Normans at the battle of Brecon in 1093. The conquerors made their base on the coast at Pembroke and the castle, though fortified until the 16th century, fell to ruin.

Today the castle is represented by its original keep but surrounded by a 17th-century belvedere. It sits in an 800-acre park owned by the National Trust and embracing Newton House. This mansion was begun by the Tudor Sir Rhys ap Thomas of Carew Castle and remained in the same family (anglicized to Rice) until 1976. The present house dates from *c*1660 but was remodelled in a late-Georgian castellated style in the 1770s, after the fashion of Picton (see page 70) and Fonmon (page 88). The old village of Dinefwr was cleared and the grounds laid out on the advice, or under the influence, of Capability Brown.

Right Tudor Newton House was rebuilt in the 1660s by Sir Edward Rice after his family regained property that had been seized by Henry VIII in 1531. The oak staircase in the inner hall dates from this time.

Left The brushing room is to be found among the restored servants' quarters at Newton House. The room was set aside as an area where servants cared for boots, shoes, coats and other outdoor clothing. **Below** The wine cellar is also on view. This area may date back to the very earliest house on the site: a 16th-century survey recorded the presence of a wine cellar.

The house exterior was again altered by a later Rice in 1856. Windows were gothicized, a Venetian porch was put on the front and turrets applied to each corner. When the family could cope no more in the 1970s, Newton passed through the customary purgatory as a school, arts centre and recording studio, before mercifully passing to the National Trust in 1990.

The Trust's restoration has been superb, reviving the 17th-century decoration and furnishing the rooms to the style of *c*1912. I am less persuaded by the appearance of actors in the rooms. Whereas waxworks take the present back to the past, however artificially, actors drag the past into the present.

We are thus led through the familiar servants' quarters of brushing room, tack room, plate room and butler's sitting room. The wine cellar is splendid. Upstairs are the dining and drawing rooms, the former with a Victorian copy of a 17th-century ceiling and portraits of the Rice family down the ages. The drawing room looks out over the park beneath its original ceiling and is furnished as in 1900.

Portraits of the Talbot family, into which the Rices married in the 18th century (see Margam, page 93), line the hall and the staircase. The latter is a superb piece, original to the 17th-century house and rising three storeys. Newton is at last emerging from a long sleep, complete with service courtyards and out-buildings. The great deer park is host to a rare breed of white Dynefwr cattle.

Kidwelly castle

★ ★ Strategic Norman fortress with medieval additions

Near Kidwellly, 8 miles NW of Llanelli; Cadw, open all year

Church and castle gaze at each other across the river over the roofs of a modern village. The castle sits on a low bluff on the river Gwendraeth and seen from the right angle is one of Wales's most imposing ruins. The castle inspired one of Turner's most atmospheric watercolours.

Kidwelly was an important Norman fortress on the southern flank of 'English' Wales. It had access from the sea and guarded the Tywi estuary to Carmarthen and routes west. The first castle was rebuilt by Roger of Salisbury, appointed by Henry I to hold south Wales in 1106. The inner fortress acquired an outer ward in the 13th century and a great gatehouse in the 14th. New apartments were added as well as a chapel, jutting out of the castle wall towards the river. This castle was later besieged by Glyndwr, but was held with barely a dozen men. It remained in good repair throughout the Middle Ages as local headquarters of the Duchy of Lancaster. It later passed to the Earls of Cawdor, who stabilised the ruins in the 19th century.

The D-shaped castle shares with Beaumaris and Caerphilly the plan of concentric, rather than contiguous, inner and outer wards. This meant that defenders could retreat from the outer defences into what amounted to a second castle within. At Kidwelly there was a third line of defence, in that a formidable main gatehouse, as at Chepstow, formed part of the outer wall yet was linked to the inner, so that it could be defended independently of the other two 'castles'. Before the invention of artillery this was a fortress of immense strength.

The building today is entered between the towers of the gatehouse, with twin portcullises and murder holes. The inner castle has four towers and walls intact. The masonry indicates where they were heightened at the time of the building of the outer wall, so they could see over it. Little of the interior remains, though the roofless chapel with a chamber for a priest is clearly identifiable, as are the guardrooms in the towers.

'... this was a fortress **of immense strength.'**

Lampeter: St David's College

★★ The earliest Welsh university buildings

College Street, Lampeter; private house, open by arrangement

Lampeter was Wales's first university, indeed the first in Britain after Oxford and Cambridge. It was planned by Bishop Burgess in 1806 as a college for training Welsh priests under the auspices of St Davids. The original location was to be Llandewi Brefi, to designs allegedly by John Nash.

The offer of a site in the old Norman borough of Lampeter by a Bristol banker, J. S. Harford, led to a change. C. R. Cockerell was commissioned and produced what was, in essence, an Oxford college quadrangle. The college opened in 1822. Though its students expanded beyond Anglican ordinands, it did not become a part of the University of Wales until 1971.

The old college, embraced by modern extensions, retains its Regency-gothic appearance. A castellated two-storey façade has a central gatehouse and tower with two projecting wings in Tudor-gothic. Beyond lies a quadrangle with cloister (now glazed), hall and chapel, adorned with a statue of St David. The walls are partly rendered and the windows are iron-framed. The chapel was altered by T. G. Jackson, architect of Oxford's 19th-century Jacobean revival, with later fittings by Caroe.

Lampeter is rightly proud of its library, built round 22,000 books acquired almost at random and donated in 1834 by an East India surgeon, Thomas Phillips. To this has been added a collection of early religious tracts together with three Hebrew scrolls and eight medieval manuscripts. The whole ensemble forms a charming encounter in this secluded corner.

LAUGHARNE

The Castle

LAUGHARNE

 A seaside castle converted into an Elizabethan mansion

King Street, Laugharne; Cadw, open part year

Laugharne vies with Solva and Oxwich among the scenic delights of the south Welsh coast. In the Middle Ages it attracted military attention and now attracts Dylan Thomas devotees. The castle was occupied by Lord Rhys of Deheubarth and the Llywelyns until rebuilt by the de Brian family, whose two giant round towers stand, as majestic from below today as in Turner's watercolour of the scene. The castle was granted to the Percys, Earls of Northumberland, during the Wars of the Roses.

Laugharne's present character was determined by its 16th-century rebuilding by Sir John Perrot, Elizabethan adventurer (possibly the queen's half brother) and rebuilder of Carew. He converted it into a residential mansion complete with formal garden. The castle fell into ruin but the grounds were turned into ornamental gardens and the site today is more picturesque than military; witness its magnificent cedar.

Laugharne has received much attention from archaeologists (with nine pages in Pevsner), seeking to distinguish military from domestic work. This is near meaningless to the visitor, for whom the ancient walls seem all of apiece. The outer gatehouse gives onto the gardens, with the ruins of the house and the inner ward ahead. Here the round towers of the medieval structure are linked by the gentler buildings of Perrot's additions, including a stately staircase turret. The inner ward is surrounded by the great hall and offices of the mansion, now reduced to bleak walls and gaping window but with glorious views over the bay.

A tower overlooking the garden has been converted into a gazebo. Here the author, Richard Hughes, who rented the castle between the wars, wrote many of his novels. A stream and ancient bridge lie immediately below.

Dylan Thomas's house

 Boathouse refuge of the great Welsh poet

Dylan's Walk, Laugharne; private house, open all year

A short walk along the coast path east of the village leads to the garage and old boathouse in which Dylan Thomas spent the four years before his death in 1953. The boathouse was put at the 35-year-old Thomas's disposal by Margaret Taylor, wife of the historian, A. J. P. Taylor. It was no small kindness as Thomas had a wife and three young children and his chronic indebtedness made it unlikely that he would leave.

Here in the gentle seaside village that he both loved and hated Thomas found a sort of contentment, writing copiously and producing his 'voice play', *Under Milk Wood*, a satire on the daily life and gossip of Laugharne (christened Llareggub). He recorded the dark net-curtained half-secrets of people 'who you can see any day of the week, slowly, dopily wandering up and down the streets like Welsh opium-eaters.' The village wears its celebrity light and the pubs eschew 'Thomas drank here' signs.

The 19th-century boathouse is preserved to excess as a shrine, under siege from tourists. It has been converted into a souvenir shop above and tearoom below, so that only the sitting room remains of the Thomas period. This preserves a sense of 1950s' petit bourgeoisie, from which Thomas was clearly unable to detach himself. It has furniture of the period, armchairs, antimacassars, a gramophone and copies of the *Illustrated London News*. There are pictures of Thomas's all-suffering wife, Caitlin. Even this idyllic setting could not calm a relationship that she called sheer hell, 'raw, red, bleeding meat'.

The setting fed Thomas's sonorous metaphors with its view over the estuary marshes and its cries of seabirds: 'Under and round him go /Flounders, gulls, on the cold, dying trails'. The house is enlivened by a tape of Thomas's rich 'old port wine' voice, reading his lines as if over an old radio.

LAUGHARNE

Above About a hundred yards from the boathouse is Dylan Thomas's writing shed. It was built in the 1920s by Dr Cowan, a previous inhabitant of the boathouse, as a garage to house his Wolsey car. The anthracite stove was added when Thomas took it over as a study.

Sound is a sensation so often missing from historic buildings. It is good to have an excuse for it here.

Back along the path is the garage, a poet's study as he left it, visible only through a window. This is an inspired work of conservation. It appears that nothing has been touched. Everything is a mess. Scribbled and screwed up paper litters the floor. Newspapers lie everywhere. A bottle of beer stands next to an inkwell. An old jacket is over a chair (added, I notice, since Peter Segar's 1990 photograph). Pictures are pinned to the walls, including one of D. H. Lawrence and another of a Modigliani. There is dust everywhere. It would give a National Trust housekeeper a fit.

Dylan Thomas
1914–53

Born in Swansea in October 1914, Dylan Thomas began his writing career as a journalist, aged just 16. But it was poetry that he loved, moving to London in 1934 to pursue his literary goals. By 1949, when he and his wife moved into the boathouse in Laugharne, Thomas was an acclaimed poet. He died in 1953, of alcohol poisoning, while in the USA for the first performance of *Under Milk Wood*.

Llanerchaeron

★★★ House and self-sufficient estate preserved from early 19th century

Near Cilau Aeron, 15 miles SW of Aberystwyth; National Trust, open part year

The villa sits in a secret valley inland from Aberaeron and is an early work of John Nash, marrying architecture to landscape. Nash had just escaped bankruptcy after a disastrous theatrical career in Carmarthen and was struggling to reinvent himself. The result was a dozen villas in the Aberystwyth district, of which only Llanerchaeron survives in its original form.

We owe this to the house's other quality, the unfaltering continuity of a Welsh gentry family, the Lewises. They were deliberately self-sufficient, married locally, hunted, fished, remained unobtrusive and content in their lot. Their antecedents, the Parrys, had lived in the Aeron valley since the 17th century. A Colonel William Lewis commissioned Nash in the early 1790s, by when he had already built Llanfechan (now demolished) nearby. Nash produced a simple villa, now yellow pebble-dashed, that would not look out of place in London's Regent's Park.

Lewis's daughter-in-law, Mary Lewis, lived at the house until her death at 104 in 1917, presiding over the estate and permitting none of the alterations seen in most Victorian houses. It was a homely property with Georgian domestic offices round a rear courtyard. Lewis's great-nephew succeeded her and lived at Llanerchaeron as squire until 1989, after which it passed to the National Trust. By then it has seen just three conservative occupants since construction

The Trust struggled to revive the garden, but only a £1m bequest rescued the house and opened it to the public in 2004. What could be found of the family's collection was recovered and much else was acquired. That said, Llanerchaeron suffers from the Trust's inability to give its properties a sense of habitation. The house needs a resident, a child, a dog, a bit of clutter, even a speck of dust.

'The villa sits in **a secret valley ... marrying** architecture to landscape.'

Above left The morning room was updated in the 1920s when the picture rail and contemporary grate were added. The Trust have refurnished the room in mid-20th-century style. **Above right** Few of the original fittings of the kitchen survive and it is now furnished with items and objects on loan from the Ceredigion Museum and the Geler Jones Collection.

The exterior is handsome rather than uplifting, a formal box with shallow hipped roofs and deep Regency eaves. Curved arches surmount the ground floor windows and Doric door surround. The interior is modest but beautifully proportioned, the hall framed by shallow arches leading to a staircase with conical roof-light. Nash took great trouble over his cornices and friezes, as if eager to break out of the minimalism of the Regency villa style. The walls are covered in trophies not of the grand chase but of the wildlife of a Welsh valley, mostly foxes, badgers, stoats, otters and fish, some startlingly ferocious.

The furnishings are, by contrast, mostly early 20th century. The result is an eclectic jumble of mantelpieces, tables and chairs that can jar with their settings. The ubiquitous group portraits and hunting prints (which seem to outnumber books in the 'library') make the rooms seem Victorian rather than Georgian. The Lewis family may have passed on but their faces are everywhere.

The presentation of bedrooms and bathroom upstairs is immaculate. The main rooms are separated by delightful oval boudoirs. A fire-screen in one is adorned with early theatrical photographs. The curved dressing room is Nash at his most sophisticated, with the tables and basins fitted into niches.

Two rooms have been converted, somewhat eccentrically, to house a collection donated to the Trust by Pamela Ward, a Kensington antiques dealer, in 1994. It comprises some 5,000 pieces mostly of up-market junk, referred to as of 'high decorative quality': toys, corkscrews, children's books, stickers, mugs and fans, including the 'language of the fan'.

Llanerchaeron is especially proud of its service quarters, which survived into the 1980s devoid of 19th or 20th-century technology (other than electricity). Here are a kitchen, beer cellar, pantry, scullery, larder, laundry, dairy, cheese press, smoke house and salting room, the entire battery of rural self-sufficiency. For some reason 'the cooks were always English or Scottish'. At the end of the servants' range is a Victorian billiard room.

The house has a generous kitchen garden whose produce is on sale to visitors. Beyond is a home farm, again largely unaltered and restored by the Trust.

Manorbier castle

★★ Picturesque castle overlooking a bay, birthplace of Gerald of Wales

At Manorbier, 5 miles SW of Tenby; private house, open part year

Just as Laugharne is forever Thomas so Manorbier is Gerald of Wales, the first British writer with a sense of authorial personality. The son of a Norman colonist who settled in Manorbier and of Princess Nest's daughter, Angharad, he was thus a commentator on 12th-century Wales acutely aware of his dual nationality, 'too Welsh to be Norman and too Norman to be Welsh,' he wrote (in Latin).

Gerald deplored the Welsh custom of reducing every argument to a battle and the Welsh inclination 'to avenge not only recent but ancient affronts.' Yet he constantly pushed the Welsh cause and was to become a patron saint of Welsh nationalism. Sent for his education to France, Gerald's one ambition was to become Bishop of St David's and make the diocese a Welsh archbishopric separate from Canterbury. He was unashamed in his self-promotion, describing himself as tall, handsome, a magnificent horseman and talented scholar. But Welsh autonomy of any sort was anathema to the Normans and Gerald's cause was doomed to failure.

In 1188 Gerald travelled the length of Wales, accompanying Archbishop Baldwin of Canterbury to raise money and troops for the Third Crusade. The journey yielded the first great work of British topography, the *Journey through Wales*. It referred to everything from nature, the weather and the

'... the pleasantest spot in the country.'

Gerald of Wales

diet of the people to the (Norman) laxity of the monasteries visited. Gerald declared that 'you will never find anyone worse than a bad Welshman, but you will certainly never find any better than a good one.' He added, 'When I see injustice in either race I hate it.'

On one topic Gerald would brook no argument, Manorbier was 'the pleasantest spot in the country.' He might well say the same today. The castle in which he was presumably born sits on a bluff separating the village from the beach, facing the church across a narrow valley filled with a dribble of roofs and car parks.

This was the home of the Norman de Barri family and, as it seems to have held little military value, the de Barris retained it with comparative ease for two centuries. In the 1600s it was acquired from the Crown by the Philipps family, who own it to this day. It was leased by the Victorian antiquarian, J. R. Cobb (see Caldicot, page 104, and Pembroke, page 68), who repaired some of the floors and roofs and built a house in the inner ward.

The composition is most attractive, a castle wall without a keep but lined with domestic buildings, including a gatehouse, hall and chapel. The last retains its barrel vault intact above traces of a later fireplace. There are also basements, corridors and tower chambers in which the owners have made an attempt at bringing a medieval castle to life. There is even a waxwork of Gerald. The presence of a holiday home within the walls adds a touch of humanity to this happy ensemble.

Nanteos mansion

★★☆ Romantic house and reputed former home of the Holy Grail

1 miles S of Aberystwyth; private house, open by arrangement but temporarily closed for restoration – expected to reopen in summer 2009

Was *Parsifal* composed in Wales? Nanteos played host to Wagner and is fabled as the home, for four centuries, of the 'Holy Grail'. Legend holds that the cup used at the Last Supper was entrusted to Joseph of Arimathaea, who brought it to his alleged foundation of Glastonbury in Somerset. With the impending dissolution of the monasteries in the 16th century the Grail was carried to Strata Florida, on whose dissolution it was carried over the hills to Nanteos outside Aberystwyth. The Nanteos Cup certainly exists and is a battered wooden bowl four inches wide with many chips out of it, probably medieval. It was eagerly sought for its miraculous healing powers, and remained at Nanteos into the 1960s. It is now thought to be with the Mirylees, cousins who inherited when the last Powell died in 1950.

The house is charming shabby-genteel, set in the secluded Paith valley. Seat of the Powells throughout history, it was rebuilt by them in 1739 as a result of the marriage of two families who lived on either side of the valley, the Powells, rich from lead mining, and the Joneses. In the late 19th century Nanteos was the home of George Powell, eccentric poet, Icelandic scholar and music-lover. It was he who invited Wagner to stay at the time of the composition of *Parsifal*, so a local inspiration is not implausible. The house was sold in 1967. It was bought by the Bliss family in 1959 and opened as a craft centre, then a wedding and bed and breakfast venue. The current owners, the Lipscombes, bought the house in 2004 and are nobly seeking to restore its old glory. There is about it a sense of grandeur anticipated and not realized.

The building is essentially Georgian, though the façade has a later centrepiece, with a Doric porch and tall arched windows. More curious are the baroque window pediments. These ostensibly

Above The music room at Nanteos is lavishly adorned with rococo decoration; an oval mirror above the fireplace is surrounded by sinuous forms and draped with an extravagant swag.

17th-century features were added later as decoration. The Pevsner authors suggest that their additional use on the side walls suggests that the architect 'had unwillingly to find place for 14 pediments and chose to use as few as possible on his main façade.'

The interior had, at the time of writing, lost much of its residential character. The entrance hall and staircase are grand, if sparsely furnished. The former drawing room, dining room and library are allocated to meetings, but benefit from the presence of reputedly Powell portraits. The stairs rise spaciously on treads of Welsh oak to a fine upstairs gallery/corridor, lined with pillars and pediments. Painted glass depicts the arms of the Powells.

The jewel of Nanteos is the middle room on the first floor, the rococo music room. Here Gruffydd Evan played the harp for 69 years and here, so it is said, Wagner did some of his composing. The room is a thrilling experience. The rococo ceiling, frieze and overmantel drip with ribbons, tendrils and sprays of fruit and flowers. Painted columns support a screen in front of the entrance, while curtains guard the windows. Candle-lit at night and with the sound of harp and piano carried out over the valley this must have been a place of special magic.

Nanteos possesses magnificent stables, worthy of Vanbrugh. At the time of writing they are lost in vegetation, pleading for restoration. The whole Nanteos ensemble is the walking wounded of the catastrophe of Welsh house conservation in the 20th century. Happier days must lie ahead.

Pembroke castle

⭐⭐⭐ Grim Norman fortress with round keep

At Pembroke, 9 miles W of of Tenby; private house, open all year

At the time of the conquest, William I was content to leave the king of Deheubarth, Rhys ap Tewdwr, alone at Dinefwr and leave Wales to its feuding princes. The policy did not outlast William's death. In 1093 Roger of Montgomery, Earl of Shrewsbury, and his son, Arnulf, crossed into Wales from their base in the central Marches and swept all before them.

Pembroke castle soon established itself as the strongest fortress in the south-west, both asserting Norman supremacy and protecting the sea route to Ireland. In 1105 Gerald of Windsor was sent as constable, with Rhys's orphaned daughter, Princess Nest, as his wife, a symbol of the Normans' desire to forge bonds with local chieftains. From the mid-12th to the mid-13th century, Pembroke was held

'... the view upwards from within echoes to the fury of Norman power.'

first by the de Clares and then by the 'king' of the Marches, William Marshall and his descendants.

Marshall's story is almost as spectacular as Nest's. A young adventurer at Henry II's court, he in 1189 unhorsed the king's rebellious son and heir, Richard (later Lionheart), in a skirmish but spared his life. Richard rewarded him with the daughter of Richard 'Strongbow' de Clare, heiress to estates in Wales and Ireland.

From 1204 Marshall rebuilt the two greatest castles in south Wales, at Chepstow and Pembroke, and secured dominance over the whole region. Pembroke, like Berwick, enjoyed semi-autonomous 'palatinate' power, so decisions could be taken quickly against an ever-threatening enemy. A line of lesser castles was built across mid-Pembrokeshire and the southern half of the present county was colonized by English and Flemish settlers.

The castle today is most impressive from outside, since Marshall's walls appear to stand virtually intact. In the Civil War Pembroke declared for Parliament but, as so often in Wales, the occupiers switched to the Royalists just when the latter faced defeat. Cromwell personally supervised the only concerted assault the castle ever faced. He cut off its water supply and promised its defenders safe passage. To ensure no further trouble he demolished the outer walls of all the towers and the great gatehouse.

What is seen today owes much to 19th and early 20th century reconstruction, first in the hands of the antiquarian, J. R. Cobb, who bought it in 1879, and then of the Philipps family, which owns it to this day. Cobb and the Philippses were equally active at Manorbier (see page 64). Towers were rebuilt and floors and chimneys inserted.

A parade ground has been laid down in the vast outer ward where, on my last visit, a detachment of redcoats were preparing to do battle in the pouring rain.

The castle comprises a spacious outer ward and, at its seaward side, a mostly destroyed inner ward. The latter is dominated by Marshall's circular Norman keep of c1204, the largest and most impressive of its period in Britain. To Jan Morris it is 'the most frightening thing in Wales … in the nastiest castle.' The keep rises 75 feet, with a battered base 20 feet thick, enclosing four storeys reached by a single spiral staircase. From its domed summit a view can be had over the Pembroke River towards Milford Haven. Although all the floors have gone (or not been reinstated) the view upwards from within echoes to the fury of Norman power.

Next to the keep is a dungeon tower, with a waxworks prisoner visible through a glass trapdoor. The ruins of a great hall and chapel survive, while beneath lies the Wogan Cave, a large natural cavern that also served as a boathouse. Remains found inside date back to the Stone Age.

Picton castle

✩✩✩ Ancestral seat with medieval remains beneath a Georgian superstructure

3 miles E of Haverfordwest; private house, open part year

Picton has been the seat of the Philipps family since the time of James I, from whom John Philipps bought a baronetcy for £1,095. He himself was a descendant of Sir John Wogan, who held the castle here as early as 1301. Philippses have thus been squirearchs of Pembrokeshire for seven centuries. They were prominent in helping rescue many of the county's castles (see Pembroke, page 68, and Manorbier, page 64) and still live on the estate.

The castle well illustrates the evolution of a Marcher property down the ages, from medieval fortress to Victorian mansion. The result may seem eccentric. There is something unreal about Picton, as if each of its features were pretending to be something else, reality parading as a sham.

Yet real it is. Wogan's medieval castle was a rectangle of four round towers protecting a great hall between them, as opposed to the familiar inner and outer wards of most Welsh castles. Fragments of this structure survive in the basement where there is a medieval undercroft with the remains of the original entrance on what was formerly the ground floor.

The Philipps conversion in the 18th century was dramatic. It involved building a causeway up to the present first-floor entrance between two of the towers, enabling visitors to enter the main rooms on what was a *piano nobile*. These rooms were converted into the apartments seen today.

Then in 1800 the new Lord Milford drastically altered the appearance and balance of the house by demolishing the far end and building a castellated block with additional rooms, as befitting a newly ennobled magnate. These included a drawing room, dining room and bedrooms. The whole was then rendered and painted white, turning a dark fortress into a Regency medieval fantasy. This effect has since been lessened by the removal of some of the render.

As a result of these changes, a wander round the house is to pass back and forth in time. The core of the house remains the hall, fashioned in the mid-18th century, on which James Gibbs was reputedly consulted. Deeply set arched windows shed light on a classical interior, pink walled, warmly furnished and hung with family portraits. At the entrance end is a balustraded gallery on fluted Doric columns, above which rises one of only four Snetzler organs extant. The stone fireplace by Henry Cheere indicates Philipps's determination that nothing but the best would do for a gentleman's house, wherever it should be.

The Georgian domestic rooms are located in the round towers, the delicacy of their decoration contrasting with the formidable depth of their walls. The library is the finest of these, with curved bookshelves, secret panels and even a curved door, carpentry of the highest quality by James Rich of London. Most of these rooms have Cheere fireplaces. Behind the organ is the entrance to the family chapel, where the organ was previous set. It is arranged with box pews against the side walls and a stained glass window behind the altar.

A corridor beyond the hall leads to the 1800s wing, past a Philipps family tree of impressive pedigree. The Regency dining room is boldly painted in deep blue and white with elaborate plasterwork over the doors. The portraits are mostly of the family of the Victorian Sir James Philipps, one of whose 13 children was able to revive the title of Lord Milford. He had later to purchase Picton from another branch of the family to whom it had descended.

The medieval undercroft, splendidly vaulted, now contains family impedimenta as well as the original entrance, including arrow slits and marks of the portcullis mountings.

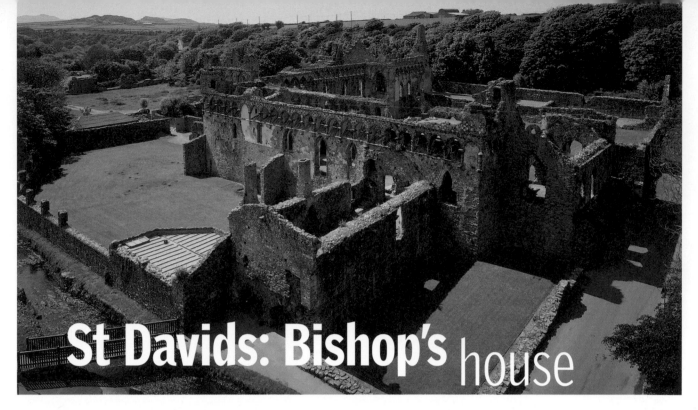

St Davids: Bishop's house

⭐⭐ Episcopal residence with two halls and mural decoration

The Close, St Davids; Cadw, open all year

The palace sits downhill from the cathedral but as architecture it is superior. It was built by the Normans and entertained Henry II and Archbishop Baldwin on his tour with Gerald of Wales. The glory days were those of Bishop Gower in the mid-14th century. Gower's work was so extensive – the hall is one of the biggest in Britain – that little by way of addition was later required. St Davids is thus a rare, virtually complete palace of the pre-Perpendicular era. After Gower's death in the plague year of 1347, St Davids had no need of further magnificence and the palace entered a long decline.

The focal point of any medieval palace was the hall, centre of entertainment and symbol of earthly power. Gower was a prelate of high standing and had already been chancellor of Oxford. He clearly regarded the existing hall as inadequate and, rather than expand it, he built a separate new one. We thus see two halls on entering through the gatehouse, the earlier one on the left and Gower's hall up stairs through a porch directly ahead. These two structures form two sides of the grand courtyard. A third consists only of a vaulted undercroft.

The walls are united by a peculiar signature of Gower's work, here and at his country seat at Lamphey. This is an arcaded parapet supporting battlements in a bravura decorative programme, visible on all the roofs. The earlier Bishop's hall on the left survives complete with its undercrofts, solar, latrines and kitchen, suggesting that Gower continued to use the old hall for lesser occasions.

The porch to Gower's hall is a rich work of Decorated gothic. The steps rise beneath an ogee arch with two gabled saints' niches above. The hall itself is bare and the window tracery has gone, apart from in the rose window where it has been restored. The whole palace has a crumbling appearance, as if slightly out of focus.

Most remarkable is the wealth of surviving mural decoration. On the exterior of Gower's hall lumps of white quartz have been set into the stonework, creating a chequerboard pattern. Everywhere are carvings, mostly in the form of corbel heads. These peer down from every corner of the interior and exterior, guarding windows or lurking in vegetation. This medieval art gallery reputedly includes 170 carvings.

Tenby: Merchant's house

★★ Three-storeyed Tudor townhouse, immaculately restored

Quay Hill, Tenby; National Trust, open part year

Tenby is an enchanting resort. While 19th-century esplanades crown its bluffs, tiny lanes lead down to the quayside and the boats to Caldey. Only the ruined Victorian fort on the promontory is an eyesore, and that can be rescued.

The old merchant's house would once have been among hundreds. It is of stone and dates from the late-15th century, so small that it may have embraced its neighbour. Stone built, it has just one room to each of its three floors, with a tiny herb garden to the rear.

The house is in National Trust style, with a heavy bias towards museology, though there is a splendid stuffed rat at the bottom of the latrine. The main ground-floor room would have been the merchant's shop and is filled with examples of the goods traded from south Wales, such as woollen cloth, leather, corn and fish. Imports were wine, spices and salt. The room contains old Welsh chests. To the rear is the kitchen and large chimney range.

The first floor acted as hall and living room, at one point connected with the house next door. In one corner is the latrine tower, illuminated, with an explanation of how it 'worked'. Clothes were hung above it so the stink could kill fleas – hence the name garderobe for lavatory. The room contains more Welsh furniture. On the wall is a modern tapestry of Tenby in 1991 by Ruth Harries. The tiny herb garden has been replanted but sadly not for visitors' use.

Above left The Merchant's House is the oldest furnished residence in Tenby and its rooms, including the second-floor bedroom, have been re-created by the Trust to reflect the lifestyle of a prosperous Tudor merchant and his family

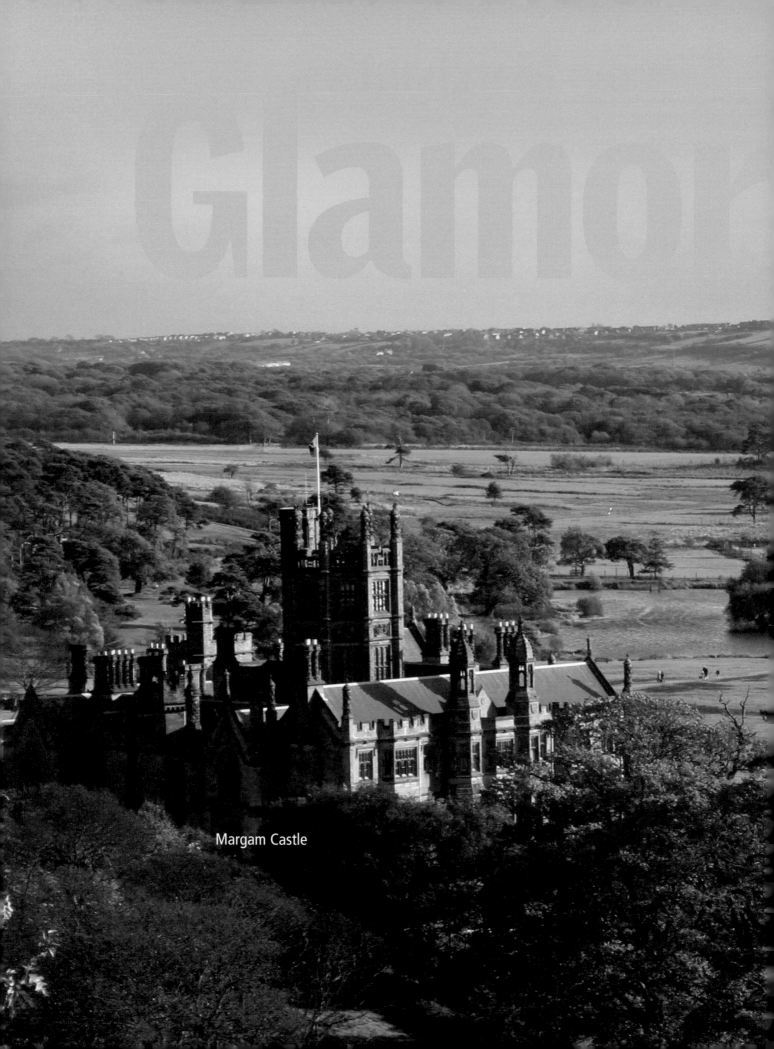

Margam Castle

Glamorgan

Caerphilly castle

★★☆ Formidable fortress set within moats, now surrounded by a municipal park

At Caerphilly, 6 miles N of Cardiff; Cadw, open all year

Henry III's Treaty of Montgomery of 1267 briefly acknowledged Llywelyn (the Last) as effective king of Wales after the most successful campaign against the English of any Welsh leader. Llywelyn's territory included virtually all of present-day Wales apart from the southern strip of the Marches. The Marcher lords were on the run and Henry, hard-pressed by Simon de Montfort in England, was forced to acknowledge it.

Of the still resisting lords, Gilbert de Clare of Glamorgan did not sit and wait. A year after the Treaty of Montgomery he built at Caerphilly one of the most impressive fortresses not just in Wales but, claim its admirers, 'in the western world'. The only explanation for its modern obscurity is that it now stands in a dull town north of Cardiff. Its surrounding municipal park no longer besieges it, but rather bores

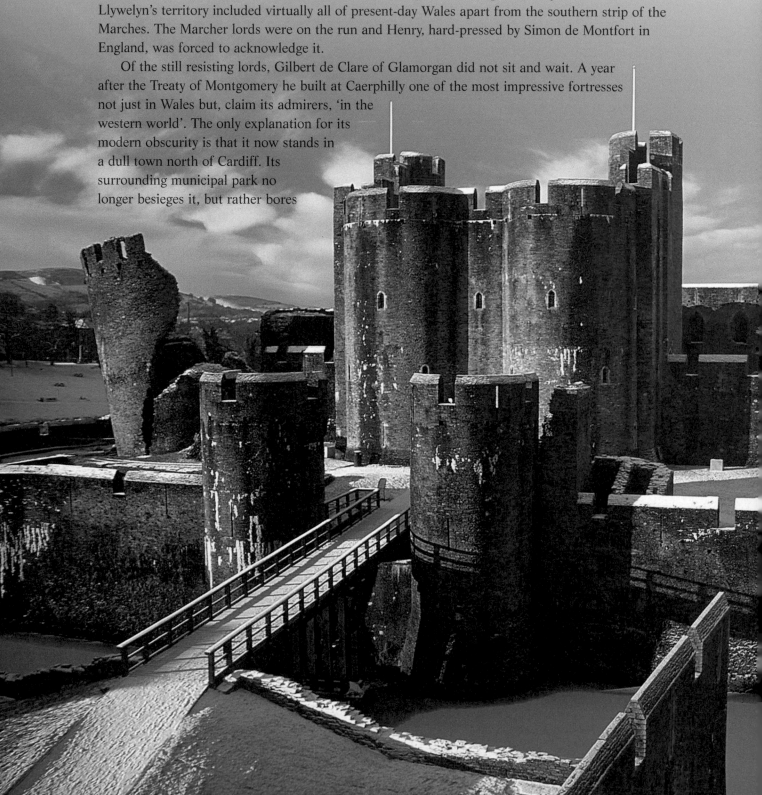

it into submission. Since it was built on flat land, topography lends it neither distance nor romance. Yet Caerphilly's walls, moats and gatehouses form a fortress comparable only with Dover Castle.

The castle was begun in 1268 and modelled on Kenilworth, where Simon de Montfort's forces had recently been defeated. De Clare noted that at Kenilworth lakes had been as effective as walls or contours in fending off attack. Water rendered ladders, catapults and wall-sapping ineffective and approach across water was hard to conceal. Caerphilly's network of concentric waterworks and walls thus presented assailants with multiple obstacles, and defenders with multiple vantage points.

De Clare lost Caerphilly briefly to Llywelyn's resurgent revolt, but it was recaptured and

reinforced, later passing to Richard II's favourite, Hugh le Despenser. Only when Marcher power in Glamorgan was concentrated on Cardiff, did Caerphilly fall into decay. Its stone was used as a quarry and one of its towers subsided into the marshy ground. But its splendour did not escape the ever-attentive Marquesses of Bute. They removed houses that had invaded the site, reroofed the Great Hall and rebuilt walls and towers where it was clear how they had fallen, using original masonry or, in some places, early concrete.

The approach today is as was originally intended, the drained moats being re-flooded in the 1950s. A mighty curtain wall faces the visitor across a first moat, with a fortified gatehouse reached only after crossing two drawbridges. Beyond lies a second stretch of water with a second curtain wall rising directly from it. Another drawbridge must be crossed and another gatehouse/keep confronted before the inner ward is reached.

The gatehouse to this ward contains the chambers of the constable of the castle and is in every sense the *piece de resistance*. The gatehouse rooms are guarded by two massive doors and reached up a spiral staircase with arrow-slit windows. The interior was reconstructed by Bute, including a great chamber and chapel.

The inner ward is that of a conventional 13th-century castle, with defensive towers and turrets round the walls and a Great Hall to one side. Remodelled by Despenser in the 1320s, this hall has been restored close to its original form and is most impressive. The roof rests on capitals depicting Edward II and his queen. The windows are Decorated gothic with ball-flower decoration.

I last saw Caerphilly on a spring evening when it was being prepared for jousting and feasting, of the sort much ridiculed by purists. If the Victorians could recreate with such care the fabric of these places, why should we not recreate the spirit in which they were used?

Cardiff castle

★★★★ Victorian Gothic masterpiece, created by William Burges

At Cardiff, 12 miles SE of Newport; private house, open all year

The grouping of Cardiff's civic centre is unequalled in any British city. Formed of the castle, law courts, city hall, national museum and university it is an architectural memorial to the industrial wealth once synonymous with Glamorgan. The setting of this memorial awaits rescue with increasing desperation. Cardiff Castle itself is a building of European stature, marooned behind a high wall by a moat of traffic like the Kremlin with a Hollywood make-over. The outer ward, which should be the city's central piazza, cannot even be seen without a ticket. Yet it is a remarkable collection of buildings.

The old Norman castle survives on its mound, the military headquarters of Robert of Gloucester, first Norman lord of Glamorgan. Cardiff held the key to south Wales and thus to Ireland and its custodianship passed from one Marcher lord to another, from the Despensers to the Earls of Warwick to the Earls of Pembroke. It became redundant under the Tudors and other buildings were erected to house constables and governors in more comfort along the west side of the ward.

These buildings were transformed after the marriage in 1766 of a Pembroke heiress to a Scots grandee, Lord Mountstuart, future Marquess of Bute. The Mountstuarts' principal seat was (and

Left The Summer Smoking Room is the final chamber in a suite of rooms created by William Burges in the castle's Clock Tower. A gallery runs around the top of the room, with windows looking out over the pitched roof of the tower. Burges decorated the underside of the gallery with his favourite 'jelly mould' motifs, similar to those found at Knightshayes in Devon.

'... money met art in the most fruitful alliance ...'

remains) on the Isle of Bute in Scotland and the then Marquess intended Cardiff as a residence for his son. He employed Henry Holland and Capability Brown to reorder the castle site. The Norman castle became a picturesque ruin.

Holland's house survived until the maturity of the 3rd Marquess who had succeeded to the title in 1848 at the age of just one. By now the mineral reserves of the Herbert/Bute properties in Glamorgan were soaring in value and Bute was christened 'the richest baby in Britain'. He grew up to be a retiring, aesthetic youth, obsessed with archaeology and the rituals of religion, and converting to Roman Catholicism at the age of 21. He married into the family of the Catholic Dukes of Norfolk. Bute went on to study Coptic, translate Turgenev, promote Wagner and inspire Disraeli's novel, *Lothair*. He was an echo of Bavaria's Prince Ludwig.

In 1865 when still 18, Bute met the medievalist architect, William Burges. Supremely confident in any style from Romanesque to Islamic, Burges could design a palace, a stained glass window or a set of toiletries to order. In the bonding of Bute and Burges, money met art in the most fruitful alliance in Victorian aesthetics. Nowhere was this alliance realized with such brilliance as at Cardiff.

The castle, like Bute's summer retreat at Castell Coch (see page 82), was unfinished on Burges's death in 1881. At no point did the family spend more than two months a year in Wales and descendants donated both houses to the people of Cardiff – the castle in 1947 and Castell Coch in 1950. They are admirably maintained and accessible today.

The exterior of the castle peers over the battlements of the wall that separates it from the city. Corners are adorned with watchtowers, pinnacles, flags and banners. The Clock Tower might be from Carcassonne. Next to the entrance gate is the Black Tower surviving from the medieval fortress.

Once inside the gate we see the Norman keep across the lawn, but it is the rambling composition to the left that commands attention. This comprises a 15th-century façade, rich in bay windows, sandwiched between the 18th-century Holland house and the massed towers of Burges's block on the left.

Inside, these disparate exteriors are resolved by Burges's genius, or perhaps by a conversation between Burges and Bute. There is no domesticity to Cardiff Castle, let alone any sense of functional progression. The chambers are rather distinct caskets of decorative art, objects in a museum, created with money no object.

The first group of rooms, in the Clock Tower, was built for Bute when a bachelor. The finest is the Winter Smoking Room, completed in 1872 on a theme of time. Every inch is painted with images depicting signs of the zodiac, seasons of the year, days of the week and times of the day. The huge overmantel is carved with a procession of medieval characters, hunting, wooing and sitting by the fire, carved by Burges's master-craftsman, Thomas Nicholls. They are as brightly coloured as they would have been in the 14th century.

The Bachelor's Bedroom is a celebration of the geology of Bute's wealth, though the geology is less mundane coal and iron and more precious stones from classical mythology. Here base metal becomes gold. Next to it is a bathroom lined with alabaster, with a bath imported from Rome into

Visitors now pass into the former 15th-century wing and the last work completed under Burges's personal supervision, the Arab Room. This is in blue marble with a ceiling of 'jelly-mould' vaults. It is worth trying to lie on the floor and look up at this psychedelic pattern of circles and stars. On all sides are Burges's favourite peacocks, gazing arrogantly at the fuss.

Next door is the castle's original first-floor banqueting hall, except that the Tudor original is everywhere touched with a gothic imagination. The hammer-beam roof is supported on miniature fan vaults. The murals and fireplace glorify the Norman Robert of Gloucester, depicting his castle with trumpet-blowing heralds. The other rooms continue in the same rich theme. The octagon stair has a crocodile carved on its banister, to eat any child sliding down it. The Octagon Tower beneath the flèche contains the lavish Chaucer Room, celebrating scenes from the *Canterbury Tales* beneath a ceiling of gothic Rococo. Lady Bute's contribution is said to be the eight classic heroines, 'who suffered in the cause of love'.

The Bute Tower rises to the roof garden, a Pompeiian court with surrounding peristyle and bronze fountain, alive with animals at its centre. Dappled with sunlight (if we are lucky) it is as far from the spirit of Cardiff outside as could be imagined. After this the ground-floor library, still sheltering the 3rd Marquess's leather-bound volumes, might be an anticlimax. Yet over a doorway two monkeys squabble over a book. Monkeys are everywhere.

An almost humorous shock is offered across the former entrance hall in a drawing room surviving from Holland's conversion. Plain, white and Georgian it is hung with portraits of the marquesses of Bute and appears to have been left untouched by Burges, as if in homage to his predecessor. Yet even here two monkeys lurk over a doorcase, protesting bitterly. Cardiff Castle is one long burst of exhilaration – and never without a smile.

the sides of which Burges set fishes that appear to swim when it is filled with water.

The Summer Smoking Room at the top of the tower is intended as the climax of this suite, one of the most extraordinary rooms I know. The tiled floor is based on that of the Westminster Abbey chapter house. The lower walls are lit by small windows lined with legends of the zodiac and the chimneypiece is crowned by Cupid carrying lovebirds. Below runs a frieze of medieval lovers in a wood.

In the four corners of the room are alabaster columns disappearing into giant corbels, with below them the eight classical winds. These columns support a gallery round which is a clerestory of windows beneath a dome representing the heavens. In the murals classical, gothic and metallurgical themes jostle, ablaze in gold, red and brown. The room, indeed the whole castle, refutes any claim that Victorian gothic is a grim or humourless style.

Beyond the bachelor suite is the family or guest tower. Here a children's nursery carries a frieze of characters from fairy tales, alive with Burges's invention and wit. The Bute governess was supplemented by Welsh and French maids instructed to speak to the children only in their native languages.

Castell Coch

★★★☆ Fantasy Victorian castle rising above the woods

Near Tongwynlais, 4 miles NW of Cardiff; Cadw, open all year

The site is as romantic as the imagination that exploited it. Where the River Taff shakes off suburban Cardiff and disappears into a forested ravine, rises the Welsh Neuschwanstein, dream castle of Ludwig of Bavaria. On the site of a de Clare fortress, the young 3rd Marquess of Bute in 1875 erected a summer retreat, using the same architect as was then building Cardiff Castle, William Burges. Using the old ruins as his guide, Burges produced a rich variation on his Cardiff masterpiece.

Castell Coch took many years to build and was completed only after Burges's death. It was used only briefly and occasionally by the Marquess's family before its contents were moved to Cardiff Castle. A vineyard planted on the slopes survived into the 1920s. (*Punch* declared that its wine needed four men to drink, two to hold down the drinker and another to pour it down his throat.) The building was given to the state by the Butes in 1950 and has been well restored, with the original furniture replaced.

The walk up to the castle from the valley below is a wander back through time. Bute and Burges carefully excavated, measured and recreated what they could of de Clare's ruins. Hence the basements are mostly medieval, as is the asymmetrical entrance comprising a gatehouse with working portcullis

'The walk up to the castle from the valley below is a wander back through time.'

Above The walls of the banqueting hall at Castell Coch are covered with stencil decoration and murals depicting the life and martyrdom of St Lucius and his sister, St Emerita. They were painted in 1878 by Campbell, Smith & Co, a firm of interior decorators, to designs drawn up by H. W. Lonsdale under the supervision of William Burges.

and drawbridge flanked by two towers. These have conical roofs with Bute weathervanes and cigar-like chimneys. The keep tower on the left, with its slit-eye windows, looks almost comical.

The interior courtyard has too much the image of a Robin Hood stage set. Galleries, outside stairs, windows and turrets await Douglas Fairbanks to swoop down, sword in hand. But they are an accurate medieval recreation and Burges's gothic was never meant to create a facsimile, rather a contemporary castle in the medieval style.

Only one of the four main rooms was completed by Burges in his lifetime, the banqueting hall. It is dominated by a large fireplace over which stands St Lucius, reputedly the first Christian king of Britain, with scenes from his life on the wall to the right. Overhead is a finely panelled ceiling.

Beyond is the finest of the castle's chambers, designed by Burges but completed after his death. The drawing room employs gothic as a joyful delight in nature, vibrating with colour, light and shade

and with barely an inch undecorated. The fireplace and high vaulted ceiling (which deprived the Marquess of a bedroom) were inspired by the French medieval revivalist, Viollet-le-Duc.

For crockets on the rib vaults, Burges designed butterflies. The spandrels are filled with birds flying in a starry sky. Over the chimneypiece is a gothic screen framing the three ages of man and their respective Greek gods. The walls are painted with murals depicting Aesop's fables (including a monkey with side whiskers). The roof has a central boss of a radiating sun. As the guidebook exults, this is a celebration of 'earthly creation, with the rich fertility of nature and the fragility of life symbolised by butterflies'.

Bute's bedroom is positioned over the entrance, as if to monitor his visitors. Here the stone walls and bare tiled floor seem austere. The roof is high, with a heavy tie beam and the stove/fireplace might be that of a Victorian pumping house. Burges's touch is shown in the carvings of animals and birds, in the lightness of the green and in the strange bed, half medieval, half Art Nouveau.

Lady Bute's bedroom rivals the drawing room in magnificence. The circular chamber carries stencilled blind arcading, above which rises a Moorish domed ceiling in gold and green. While the walls are medieval the ceiling is composed of panels, each decorated with flowers and animals in the

Above Among the wealth of decoration that adorns Lady Bute's bedroom is a carving of Psyche, set on the medieval-style overmantel. The winged figure, carved by Thomas Nicholls in 1887, bears the arms of Lord and Lady Bute within a heart-shaped shield. **Below** The washstand in Lady Bute's bedroom was designed by J. S. Chapple and made in 1891.

Arts-and-Crafts style. It is as if, after Burges's death, his craftsmen felt free to keep abreast of the times.

Monkeys crawl all over the place, playing with squirrels, grasping at grapes, singing the praises of nature. Nothing is left bare, not even the twin 'towers' on the washstand, dispensing hot and cold water. The extraordinary Arabic bed is supposedly a Viollet-le-Duc design. Lady Margaret's bedroom above is Spartan in comparison.

If there is sadness to Castell Coch it lies in the purposelessness of the place. Designed with exhilaration and intended for pleasure, it needs to hear music and see hospitality and entertainment, not silent groups of tourists moving quietly round hallowed halls. It cries out for an injection of life.

'The mansion ... **stands bold in its park** on the flanks of the Taff valley.'

Cyfarthfa castle

★ ☆ The castellated Regency palace of a Merthyr ironmaster

At Merthyr Tydfil, 13 miles S of Brecon; museum, open all year

The mansion of the Crawshays, kings of industrial Merthyr, stands bold in its park on the flanks of the Taff valley. Visitors must use their imagination to recapture the context in which it was built in 1824–25. William Crawshay's hard, vulgarian father bitterly opposed what he regarded as the extravagant cost of £30,000. 'A great house and an expensive establishment will not fight our battle in trade,' said the old man, probably the richest industrialist in Britain at the time.

His son William was proving an educated if flamboyant young man. On taking command of the firm he chose, unlike his father, to live opposite the family works in Merthyr in a house of his own creation. It was designed by Richard Lugar in a Regency castellated villa style on a terrace with views up and down the valley and directly opposite the Cyfarthfa works, based on the valley's astonishing reserves of coal, iron and limestone, aided by fast flowing water. At the time the house was built, this was the largest ironworks in the world, drawing thousands to the relative security of wages which, in Merthyr, tended to be above the Glamorgan average because of the higher skills required for ironworking.

The scene from the terrace at night, according to Crawshay, was 'truly magnificent … resembling the fabled Pandemonium, but upon which the eye may gaze with pleasure and the mind derive high satisfaction, knowing that several thousand persons are there constantly employed and fed by the active spirit, powerful enterprise and noble feeling of the highly respected owner.' To Thomas Carlyle, Cyfarthfa was somewhat different, 'a vision of hell'. Jan Morris later referred to it as 'a colossal detonation of smoke, steam and fire. Tall black chimneys, like etiolated tree-trunks, forcibly eject their smoke into an almost solid mass across the scene.'

Crawshay was to have three wives and 15 children and they did not enjoy living so close to so much noise and pollution. By the end of the 19th century the family had revolted against any such commitment to their home town and were living in the Home Counties. In 1909 Cyfarthfa was sold to Merthyr council.

The view from the terrace is now of modern warehouses and patches of suburban housing. The castle has been converted into a museum and gallery but traces of its residential past remain. The castellated composition is grey and unappealing, especially when compared with such contemporaries as Penrhyn (see page 150) and Gwrych (see page 28) in the north. The most prominent feature is a round tower turning the corner between the formal and service wings.

The entrance gives onto a mock medieval hall (with mock medieval sales desk). To its right are the former reception rooms, now crowded with exhibits but refurnished with wallpaper and curtains and hung with Welsh pictures and sculptures. Those on display in the morning room include works by Cedric Morris and Kyffin Williams.

The round drawing room has wallpaper by Robert Adam and cases of Wedgwood. The red drawing room is more eccentric, with a display of Egyptology and a magnificent fireplace. The dining room concentrates on portraits of the Crawshays and their factories and an exhibition of Merthyr's continuing cultural treasure, the Cyfarthfa Brass Band.

Fonmon castle

✯ ✯ ✯ Medieval tower house with Restoration wing and Rococo interiors

At Fonmon, 15 miles SW of Cardiff; private house, open part year

At first view Fonmon is an ugly duckling, misshapen, poorly crenellated and covered in streaky grey render. Inside it is quite different, an enjoyable Glamorgan gentry house with a pedigree dating back to the Norman period, kept going against all odds by descendants of its 17th-century owners.

The original fortified tower house was sited on the fertile Barry shore and protected by a steep incline to the east. The hall was on the first floor. Having survived some four centuries, the St Johns found their loyalties divided by the Civil War, a clash vividly displayed in the family mausoleum at Lydiard Tregose, in Wiltshire, with its memorial to the Golden Cavalier. The Fonmon branch, despite siding with Cromwell, sold their Welsh property in 1650 to a Parliamentarian colonel, Philip Jones.

Jones became governor of the south Welsh castles and Cromwell's chief adviser on Wales. He made his peace with Charles II after the Restoration and added a new north wing to Fonmon, with extensive offices and bedrooms. Jones's descendants, now named Boothby, have resided in the castle and cared for it to this day.

The Jones's were Baptists but this was no impediment to their status as Welsh gentry, their sons making the grand tour, collecting Panninis and forming a charming group in a painting by Hogarth. They welcomed John Wesley on his visits to Wales in the 1740s. It was then that Wesley suggested to Robert Jones that his son attend the new Methodist school at Kingswood, where a regime of puritanical asceticism was promised. It was not a good idea. Young Jones revolted, ran away from school and lived the life of a Hogarthian rake in London and Bath.

'... an enjoyable Glamorgan gentry house with a pedigree...'

Left When the library at Fonmon was created in the 1760s the work was carried out by Thomas Paty. A fellow Bristol-based craftsman, Thomas Stocking, was responsible for the plasterwork; the ceiling and arches that divide the room are decorated with fine Rococo-style motifs. Paty and Stocking collaborated on many projects, including the Royal Fort House in Bristol. Stocking also worked with Capability Brown at Corsham Court in Wiltshire.

On marrying a girl from Llantwit Major and inheriting the estate, Jones expressed his aversion to his parents' educational taste in a most emphatic way. In 1762 he commissioned the Bristol firm of Thomas Paty to convert the old castle interior into a fashionable 18th-century residence, with plasterwork by Thomas Stocking. Windows were replaced by sashes. A handsome staircase and a gallery with Rococo ceilings were created in the range linking the two main wings.

Jones next went to work on the old medieval hall. This was expanded to form a library running from front to back of the house, adorned with the finest Rococo plasterwork in Wales. At each end, arches decorated with rosettes frame Venetian windows, one of them looking down on the ravine below. Mirrored girandoles reflect candle-light from the walls. The gilt fireplace surround looks up at a ceiling that carries Rococo devices radiating from a central sun into every corner.

Of a different stamp are the service rooms, including those in the stone vaulted medieval basement. The 17th-century kitchen has a dresser filled with Jones family pewter. A photograph of a visit to the house by Queen Mary in 1938 shows the grand lady in familiarly severe mood. She is surrounded by Boothbys looking shell-shocked.

Llancaiach Fawr

★ ★ ☆ Large Tudor mansion with re-enactments of a 17th-century lifestyle

At Nelson, 12 miles NW of Cardiff; private house, open all year

Llancaiach Fawr is a spirited attempt by Rhymney Council to bring an intact Tudor house to life for visitors. It has been restored as it would have been in the time of the Prichard family, owners during the Civil War. Edward Prichard was initially a Royalist, charged with raising troops in the king's cause, but as a strong Puritan he changed sides and ended the war as the Parliamentary governor of Cardiff Castle.

The present house is staffed by actors pretending to be Prichard's servants. This is no place for those who find 'sire' and 'fare ye well' irritating or whose gorge rises on being told that the back staircase is out of bounds on account of 'God bless, but please note the health and safety features'.

Llancaiach is transitional medieval/Elizabethan. It was built in the 1530s when the old plan of a side entrance into a screens passage with hall to one side was being replaced by a central door

'... crowded with ... the clutter normal to a house of the period.'

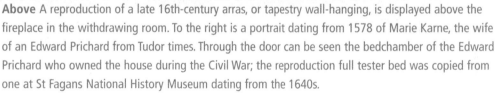

Above A reproduction of a late 16th-century arras, or tapestry wall-hanging, is displayed above the fireplace in the withdrawing room. To the right is a portrait dating from 1578 of Marie Karne, the wife of an Edward Prichard from Tudor times. Through the door can be seen the bedchamber of the Edward Prichard who owned the house during the Civil War; the reproduction full tester bed was copied from one at St Fagans National History Museum dating from the 1640s.

in a lesser receiving hall, with the formal chambers upstairs. Here the door is still to one side, but the principal family rooms are on the first floor, linked by a formal staircase only in 1628.

The archaeology of the house is thus curious. Most of the windows and possibly the porch are later additions and Newman in *Pevsner* suggests that the Elizabethan house, with its tiny windows and remarkable height, might have been designed so as to be internally defensible. The doors to the family rooms on the first floor are arranged to be heavily barred. The existence of two separate ground-floor kitchens may again be a sign of insecurity. The owner cannot have trusted even his retainers.

The house was restored and furnished in the 1980s with help from St Fagans (see page 97). The furniture is either original to the period or good reproduction. The surfaces are crowded with pewter, writing implements, hour glasses, guns, pots and pans, in other words with the clutter normal to a house of the period. The only anachronism is a metal staircase leading to the top storey, another dreaded blow from health and safety. The house has a knot garden in front and a wild garden to the rear.

Margam castle

★★★ Spectacular Victorian mansion with a celebrated orangery

Near Margam, 4 miles SE of Port Talbot; private house, open all year

Christopher Rice Mansel Talbot was a larger-than-life Victorian, descendant of the medieval Mansels of Gower (and of the Talbots of Wiltshire) and owner of a Glamorgan estate to rival that of the Butes. He was also a scholar, fellow of the Royal Society, yachtsman, Lord Lieutenant and, for 59 years, Liberal MP. His parliamentary career was distinguished by his never making a speech, except once to ask that a window be closed. Talbot gave his name to the docks at Port Talbot, which he largely rebuilt, and his private steamer was the first to pass through the Suez Canal.

On assuming his inheritance in 1813, Talbot considered his Georgian family seat at Penrice insufficiently grand. He therefore demolished the house at Margam which his family had previously left behind, and in 1830 commissioned the architect of Penrhyn, Thomas Hopper, to build him something bigger, overlooking the ruins of the old abbey. The view was superb, framed by thickly wooded hills with views over Port Talbot to the Bristol Channel and Somerset beyond.

This new house lasted barely a century. It was stripped by the family and its remaining contents sold with the Margam estate in 1942. Like so many Welsh houses, it was gutted by fire and taken over in 1977 as a roofed ruin by the local council. It has since been rescued as an education centre, its walls reduced to heart-breaking scalded brick but its windows and roofs repaired and intact.

Unlike Norman Penrhyn, Hopper gave Talbot Elizabethan at Margam, with a giant central tower and a skyline massed with battlements, chimneys and finials. The façade presents a wall of windows, adorned with every Elizabethan feature in the pattern book. Octagonal turrets have crocketed domes. Windows thrust out into oriels of varying sizes. Gables seem to rise wherever mood takes them.

The interior, for all its dereliction, retains Hopper's sense of drama, most noticeably in the stairwell. This rises on gothic arches the height of the tower to end in a tall lantern. It would make an admirable hotel, college, house, anything.

The steps in front of Margam Castle descend theatrically to the woods surrounding the old abbey. These were laid out by Mansel Talbot's Georgian predecessor, Thomas, after he had departed for Penrice. He designed the grounds as a free-standing arboretum. The ruins of the old property, such as gateposts and the magnificent renaissance façade of the banqueting house, were left as picturesque features, as was one of the largest Orangeries in Britain.

This structure, 330 feet long, was designed by Anthony Keck in 1780. The building is Palladian in design with a sculpture gallery intended at one end and a library at the other. The façade is articulated by subtle changes to the bays and roofline and by the rustication of the lower half of the wall. Venetian windows complete each end. Surrounded by pines and palm trees the building might be in the French Riviera. Nelson was so impressed by it he gave the custodian the then huge tip of three shillings. The building is used today for concerts.

Below The Orangery at Margam was commissioned by Thomas Mansel Talbot to house a collection of orange and lemon trees that he had inherited and was built between 1787 and 1793. The fashion for building orangeries on well-to-do estates was imported from the Continent, beginning in the 17th century; improvements in glass-making made it easier to design buildings with the many windows needed to make citrus cultivation possible in Britain.

Old Beaupre castle

★★ Ruined Elizabethan mansion with Renaissance porch

Near St Hilary, 12 miles SW of Cardiff; Cadw, open all year

The magic of Beaupre (pronounced Bewper and from the Norman for beautiful retreat) lies partly in its isolation and partly in its rarity. It is a magnificent relic of the Elizabethan Renaissance lost in the Welsh countryside. The house is attached to a medieval farm, reached by a half-mile footpath from a lay-by on the A48. The old 14th-century manor is still inhabited, but not the ruinous additions of the mid-16th century, begun by Sir Rice Mansel on his marriage to the heiress to the local Bassett estate. Mansel's daughter by his second wife married another Bassett and took the property with her.

Mansel formed a ceremonial forecourt to the old manorial hall, whose own courtyard remains behind. This is entered through a large fortified gatehouse with graffiti of ships on the walls. The carved date of 1586 apparently relates to Mansel's grandson, Richard Bassett, who in 1600 added the magnificent porch over the hall door on the far side of the court.

This structure is the finest work of the Elizabethan Renaissance in Wales. It is a complete 'tower of the orders', a classical composition of columns, Corinthian above Ionic above Doric. Coats of arms fill the panels and the friezes and crowning gable are richly decorated. Historians debate whether it may have come in 'kit' form from England. It certainly looks odd next to the rough Welsh chimneybreast besides which it is squeezed, and the ruined medieval hall behind.

Round the courtyard are the ghostly apartments of the Elizabethan house, bleak but still restorable. As if to prove the point, the older buildings of pre-Tudor Beaupre are in use behind, full of the bustle of a modern farm.

Oxwich castle

⭐ Fortified Tudor house, overlooking a bay

At Oxwich, 11 miles SW of Swansea; Cadw, open part year

Here is a south Welsh castle that is nothing to do with Normans, Marcher lords or rebellious Welsh. It sits overlooking the sandy and picturesque Oxwich cove where it was built by the ubiquitous Sir Rice Mansel c1520. His family had adhered to the Lancastrian cause in the wars of the Roses, shifting allegiance to the Tudors after Bosworth. Sir Rice acquired Margam abbey on the dissolution and, through his third marriage to a lady-in-waiting to Mary I, rose to become chancellor of south Wales, with permission to keep a retinue. He died in 1559. He and his son, Edward, built Oxwich and later converted the dissolved Margam abbey as a residence (see page 92).

Oxwich was thus not a fortress but rather, like Old Beaupre and Carew, the stylish house of a Tudor grandee, its gateway fortifications largely for show. Later generations made Margam their home, and later ones Penrice. The house was tenanted and finally used as part of a farm. Mansel's arms crown the entrance, flanked by the initials RM.

The earliest part of the house is the south range, to the right inside the courtyard. This is a traditional hall house with upper great chamber, now roofed and disappointingly devoted to exhibitions. The interior is a clutter of stands and displays.

Opposite the entrance is the ruin of Sir Edward's east range, once a grand structure rising four storeys, or six in the towers and built round the time of his father's death. The house had two pillar staircases, another great hall and a long gallery. It must have been as splendid as Hardwick Old Hall, in Derbyshire. Certainly it bankrupted Sir Edward.

Today all this glory is recalled only in bare walls, gaping windows, fireplaces and the gaunt ruin of one surviving tower. Outside the house enclosure is the ruin of a massive dovecote.

St Donat's castle

★ ★ Medieval castle, much restored by American press tycoon

At St Donat's, 17 miles SW of Cardiff; private house, open by arrangement

This is, or was, a precious survival of a Glamorgan fortified manor, in continuous family occupation from Norman times well into the 18th century. It is now a school, the Atlantic College, intermittently accessible but the exterior visible from the car park.

The castle's most remarkable contents came with its purchase and conversion into a Welsh San Simeon by the American press tycoon, William Randolph Hearst, in 1925. This was in honour of the supposed Welsh origins of his mistress, Marion Davies (her real name was Douras, from Brooklyn). Hearst's mostly medieval imports appear to have involved the destruction of fine houses across Britain, notably Bradenstoke Priory in Wiltshire. Hearst, or his dealers, had a good eye, though he hardly ever visited the place.

The castle lies on a hillside sloping down to the Bristol Channel with a happy outlook to Exmoor in the distance. The castle has no keep or obvious defensive efficiency. There is an outer wall with a dry moat and gatehouse, behind which rises an inner wall and another gatehouse

of Norman origins. There is hardly more than a passageway between the two walls.

Inside is a charming courtyard surrounded by a jumble of late-medieval façades, reminiscent of Berkeley Castle, Gloucestershire. These carry early Renaissance medallions apparently copied from those by Giovanni da Maiano at Hampton Court, whether original or imported from elsewhere is unclear.

To the left of the court is the entrance to the Great Hall, the fabric of which survives, including apparently some of the roof timbers. Beyond it is mostly Hearst and, as at Berkeley, there is no clear guide as to what is medieval *in situ* and what imported.

The justly named Bradenstoke Hall fills the space between the old hall and the outer curtain wall, its roof and windows from Bradenstoke and its fireplaces from France. Its windows embrace the full view downhill to the Channel. The school dining room is also a spectacular chamber, thanks to a stone screen from a West Country church, a ceiling from Lincolnshire and a chimney from France.

St Fagans National History Museum

★★★ A diverse collection of historic Welsh buildings

At St Fagans, 4 miles W of Cardiff; museum, open all year

St Fagans is the best architectural museum in Britain. It boasts over 40 buildings brought from every corner of Wales and is marred only by the bland modernity of its entrance and museum block, more an airport than a welcome to Wales's past. The site has the added attraction of St Fagans Castle, a well-restored Tudor manor with sumptuous garden.

The collection embraces a Celtic village – three dwellings re-created from actual buildings excavated in Flintshire and peopled with theatrical 'Celts' – medieval cottages, rural farmsteads, a prefab, tollbooth, pigsty, bake-house, smithy, cockpit, schoolhouse, bee-hive, shopping street, working farm and workmen's institute. The group is constantly expanding. A recent acquisition was Ty Gwyrdd, a supposedly self-sufficient modern house, using bricks and wood from the site, water from the roof and woollen insulation.

Rhyd-y-car iron worker's houses

I once took my father back to his birthplace in the Merthyr suburb of Dowlais and saw him shell-shocked at the destruction of the place. Not only had streets and houses been demolished but so had most of the public buildings of his youth. It was as if Hitler had come to the valleys, he said, to finish the job he had begun on Cardiff Docks.

The rescue in 1987 of a row of Merthyr's Georgian terrace houses (c1800) gives some sense of what has been lost. Six properties have been re-erected and displayed as each might have appeared in succeeding periods, in 1805, 1855, 1895, 1925, 1955 and (saddest of all) 1985. Their tiny gardens too can be seen changing over time, complete with rabbit hutches, pigeon houses, privies and tool-sheds.

The display is imaginative in conception and execution. Respect has been paid to the role of clutter in ordinary life: hence sewing kits, posters, unfinished meals and old newspapers. An air raid shelter is converted into a potting shed. Since the sites of so many of these terraces now lie empty one is tempted to ask, why not rebuild them *in situ* for Cardiff commuters now repopulating the valleys?

ST FAGANS

St Fagans castle

This Elizabethan house, built in the 1580s, remains on its original site. It belonged to the Lewis family who married into the family of the 18th-century Earls of Plymouth. The house was restored and 'victorianized' in the 1880s as a seat for the heir to the earldom. In 1946 the then Earl donated it to the National Museum of Wales, along with the surrounding estate. Much effort has gone into reassembling furniture appropriate to the Victorian restoration and portraits appropriate to the Plymouths.

The main façade displays the transition from medieval to Elizabethan architecture in its explicit symmetry, with a central porch and equal wings and with gables balancing the front and the sides. Yet the interior clings to the medieval past, with a screens passage, Great Hall and elaborate over-mantel.

The downstairs drawing room has another Elizabethan over-mantel, carved

Above The interiors at St Fagans Castle have been re-created as they might have appeared at the end of the 19th century. Some pieces, including the tapestries in the drawing room, remain from the castle's original furnishings.

with the Lewis arms, and a tapestry copied from a Teniers painting. The sofa cover is a patchwork stitched by Victorian house guests, while the gramophone once belonged to Adelina Patti (see Craig-y-nos, page 168). The library houses a Gillow bookcase and an enticing bottle of port.

The state bedroom contains a 1710 bed of red silk damask and embroidered wall-hangings. Panelling and fireplaces have been imported, presumably from distressed houses elsewhere in Wales, to create a sense of neo-Jacobean warmth. Even the kitchen, which in most restorations is a predictable and forlorn place, looks ready to leap into life at the mention of guests.

The castle grounds include a 1900 rose garden (with 100 varieties of rose) carefully re-created from old records and photographs. There is a rose called 'Bardou Job', thought to be extinct until rediscovered in the garden of California's Alcatraz Prison. The Italian garden has been restored and beneath it the grounds fall away dramatically to a set of ancient fishponds in a ravine.

Weobley castle

★★ Medieval castle with Elizabethan additions

Near Llanrhidian, 11 miles W of Swansea; Cadw, open all year

Weobley is the most evocative of the castles of the Gower. It had been a fortified residence since the Middle Ages and has few equals for location even among the finely positioned fortresses of south Wales. It sits on a grassy bluff looking north across the Llwchwr estuary to Llanelli and the mountains beyond. Today the castle is approached from a neighbouring farm with what seems half of south Wales spread out before it.

Begun in the early 14th century the castle was rebuilt in the late 15th by Sir Rhys ap Thomas, later passing into the ever-expanding Gower domain of the Mansels. The exterior is a mix of medieval and 16th-century work, the latter intended to convert what had been a castle into an Elizabethan mansion. Weobley would not have been hard to capture from the landward side and was presumably designed to be defensible against local troublemakers rather than play a part in a major conflict.

There is a pleasant absence of marketing clutter about the entrance, with a simple arch in the wall of the main residential block. Inside, the courtyard is a cosy jumble of façades, as if the components of a fortified manor had been compressed and squeezed upwards. To the left is the two-storey porch of the Great Hall and solar wing. To the right are service blocks and guest quarters. Almost all lack their roofs but have further views over the estuary.

'Weobley is the **most evocative** of the castles **of the Gower.'**

Gwent

Raglan Castle

Gwent

Blaenavon

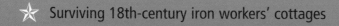 Surviving 18th-century iron workers' cottages

At Blaenavon, 8 miles SW of Abergavenny; Cadw, open part year

The rescue of traces of Blaenavon's earliest ironworks is a valiant attempt to bring the past of the valleys alive for generations that have no memory of them. So much of the blast furnace site has been destroyed that what is left, clinging to the side of a hill, is almost beyond interpretation.

Two rows of Georgian cottages, Engine Row and Stack Square, survive and these have been restored, albeit to a surreal standard of cleanliness. Philanthropists recording these dwellings in their original state emphasized their poverty and squalor, unappealing qualities to a modern curator.

The cottages in Engine Row, dating from 1788, were apparently occupied by workers imported from the Midlands, perhaps from the earlier industrial site of Shropshire's Coalbrookdale. Hence the first cottage depicts a relatively comfortable family in the 1790s, with a scattering of Shropshire furniture and prints. A replicated leg of mutton is on the table. Upstairs is the workman's Sunday best suit, his wife's best shoes and a Bible.

The second cottage is decorated as of 1841, for an Irish family in poorer circumstances. The main downstairs room is set up for clothes washing. Irish newspapers serve for wallpaper and the family sleeps on mattresses. The Catholic faith is reflected in crucifixes and rosaries. Neither cottage has sanitation and the rooms would have been coated in grime from the adjacent blast furnaces.

In 2008 three families spent a fortnight in the cottages, working in the pits and enduring the hardships of Victorian life for the benefit of a television audience. It made for a vivid documentary, an experience from which some of those involved emerged traumatized and others celebrities.

Above The first cottage in Engine Row has been recreated as the home of a foreman in the ironworks at the end of the 18th century. The rush mats, good quality furniture and handsome range, which is original to the site, all indicate a reasonably prosperous family. **Below** The second cottage has been furnished as it might have been in 1841, when furnace filler Timothy McCarthy and his family – a household of eleven – lived at Engine Row.

Caldicot castle

★★★ The remains of a medieval fortress with Victorian restorations

At Caldicot, 5 miles SW of Chepstow; private house, open part year

Caldicot is a tremendous castle but little appreciated. Though its extensive park remains intact, it sits in the ugly Gwent coastal strip, neither city nor suburb. Finding it requires an act of will. Approached through thick trees, the castle from the outside looks like a film set. It was begun on a site of a Norman motte by the Bohuns, one of the three earliest Norman Marcher lords, and extended to its present size in the 14th century. The keep, crowning the north-west of the inner bailey, is similar to those built by William Marshal at Usk (see page 118) and Pembroke (see page 68), its masonry excellently laid. The sequence of gatehouse, keep and the late 14th century Woodstock tower (named after a later owner, Thomas of Woodstock, Duke of Gloucester) contributes to one of the most impressive circumnavigations of any castle in Wales.

The reason for Caldicot's good condition is that it was bought and restored in 1884 by the antiquary, J. R. Cobb, who also restored Pembroke and Manorbier (see page 64). It passed to the council in 1963. The inner bailey is landscaped and three of the towers and some later outbuildings are in residential use. Creeper climbs up the walls and vegetation spills over the intact battlements. Ghostly fireplaces set into the bailey walls indicate residential structures now vanished.

The interiors are much as Cobb left them. The keep is in excellent condition, with domestic rooms, fireplaces and even a latrine tower. Cobb converted the gatehouse with its upper hall into a house and this is now used for entertainments, weddings and banquets. The central bailey is open for jousts. Flowers and trees are everywhere.

Right The great gatehouse at Caldicot was built by Thomas Woodstock in the late 14th century and is still entered over a drawbridge. The residential buildings created by J. R. Cobb can clearly be seen on the inner side of the gatehouse (below). These were divided into apartments and let out until the 1960s.

'... the castle **from the outside** looks like **a film set.**'

Chepstow castle

★ ★ The greatest Norman fortress in south Wales

At Chepstow, 17 miles NE of Newport; Cadw, open all year

The castle is the glory of medieval south Wales, overlooking the final bend in the River Wye as it joins the Severn. It was the first of the fortresses built by the Normans to contain the Welsh, begun within a year of the Battle of Hastings. Today it has lost much of its menace and spreads itself along a limestone cliff like a Siamese cat resting in the sun.

Chepstow's walls, keep and gatehouse, its four baileys and Great Hall are everything a model castle should be. If it suffers from over-scraping – compared with Turner's romantic depiction in 1793 – there is a delightful whisper of wallflower and rosebay willowherb on the battlements and the view from the bastions over the river is placid and sylvan.

'... [the castle] **spreads itself** along a limestone cliff like a **Siamese cat resting in the sun.'**

Chepstow and the Saxon earldom of Hereford were awarded by the Conqueror to his most loyal follower, William FitzOsbern, partly in return for his fealty and partly to guard against 'the bellicose Welsh'. Begun in 1067 the square keep was one of the first stone castles in Britain, one of a line of defences (initially of earth and wood) along Offa's Dyke and including Monmouth, Hereford and Ludlow. FitzOsbern died within a decade and his son forfeited his inheritance through treachery.

The land and castle passed in *c*1115 to another Marcher grandee, Walter de Clare, and by marriage to the glamorous William Marshal. This 'flower of chivalry', soldier, jouster and Jerusalem pilgrim was premier courtier to Henry II and Eleanor of Aquitaine. He later negotiated the Magna Carta for King John and was regent of England during the minority of Henry III. He died in 1219, lord of Pembroke and Usk as well as Chepstow. His prominence in Welsh history is a measure of the threat Wales posed to the Normans.

Marshal's descendants held the castle through the 13th century, converting it from a tower on a cliff to the castle we see today. The grandest, Roger Bigod, Earl of Norfolk and Earl Marshall of England, appears to have made it his principal residence, doubling the size of the Norman tower and creating an extensive early medieval palace in the lower bailey. By the time of the Tudors, Chepstow had joined Raglan in the domain of the Earls of Pembroke and Worcester, eventually Dukes of Beaufort.

Only with the Tudor accession did these mighty castles decline, briefly returning to life during the Civil War. Even as a ruin Chepstow retained its magnificence into the 18th century, and with the celebration of the Wye as a tourist destination under the Regency, it was seen as the embodiment of romantic Wales. It was the first castle to be used as a film set, for Ivanhoe in 1913.

The approach is up a steep lawn above which rise the massive 13th-century Marten's Tower on the left and Marshal's Norman gatehouse. Together with their adjoining walls they form as imposing a composition as any in Britain. Immediately inside the gatehouse are Roger Bigod's later domestic buildings, including chambers for his knights and servants, the great kitchen range and the gloriette, or private wing, with dining hall and views over the Wye valley. This is in a good state of preservation in part because it was still inhabited into the 19th century.

The interior of Chepstow continues with three further baileys or courtyards, each with a distinctive character and purpose. The middle bailey leads uphill to the original Norman hall or Great Tower. This was almost certainly intended as William the Conqueror's base in south Wales even if he did not use it. There is a Norman arch and some wall paintings, said to be the earliest domestic decoration in Britain. The upper part was rebuilt by Marshal and then by Bigod; some of Marshal's gothic vaulting survives and is of high quality.

Beyond these domestic quarters the castle becomes a rambling series of walls, openings and obscure footings. The walls offer exhilarating walks with views towards both the town and the river.

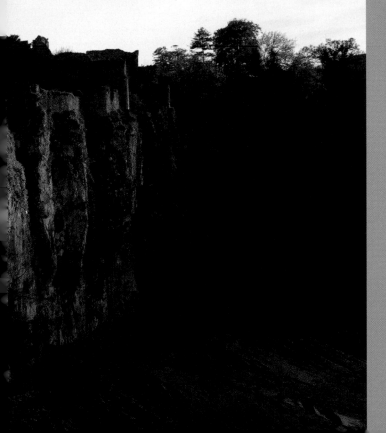

Clytha castle

★ Gothick folly in picturesque setting on a hill

Near Bettws Newydd, 5 miles SE of Abergavenny; private house, open by arrangement

Clytha is an artful landscape of the sort that once abounded in Wales, mostly reduced to such ghosts as Hafodunas (see page 30) and Gwrych (see page 28). As we pass up the Usk valley along the eastern flank of the Black Mountains, the landscape briefly mellows. Slopes, trees and meadows appear to come to order as if in response to the hand of man, which is what has indeed happened.

In 1790 a local landowner, William Jones, decided to commemorate his beloved but departed partner, Elizabeth, with a gothick folly on a prominent hill a mile from his seat at Clytha Park. It was to be a banqueting house dedicated, says a plaque on the exterior, to 'the purpose of relieving a mind afflicted by the loss of a most excellent wife.'

That consolation is spectacular. Castellated turrets start up from the trees (of which there are now too many) as from a fairy castle. The building is formed as two sides of a sham castle, plastered with a pink wash, with two fake towers and one inhabited. These are linked by a swooping concave parapet. The whole is embattled and studded with arrow slits, overstated but designed to be seen from a distance. It was this that caused John Loudon, historian of the picturesque, to dismiss Clytha as 'gaudy and affectedly common'.

Guests would have enjoyed views across the valley to the Skirrid and Sugar Loaf mountains. Though the house belongs to the Landmark Trust (and can be rented) it is accessible from the surrounding National Trust parkland. Jones's heir, also William, converted Clytha Park in the 1820s into an anything-but-gothick Greek revival house, designed by Edward Haycock of Shrewsbury. This is visible from the main road through a jolly arch. Its Bath stone Doric portico displays a stern austerity contrasting with the castle on the hill.

Llanvihangel court

★★★ Ancient Tudor house with original 17th-century stables

4 miles N of Abergavenny; private house, open part year

This is a heart-warming place, a well-restored Elizabethan/Jacobean mansion safe in private hands and accessible to public view. The old stone façade of six spacious bays gazes across the sweeping valley of the Monnow towards the English border, backed by the slopes of the Black Mountains. A painting depicts the house in the 17th century with formal avenues of the trees radiating from its terraces and the Skirrid depicted as a Welsh Table Mountain. The present owner, Julia Johnson, is replanting the avenue with Scots pines.

The entrance front is that of a Tudor mansion; the east front was rebuilt in 1559 by Rhys Morgan, a son-in-law of the mighty Herbert family. The house was 'modernized' when it was sold, first to the Earl of Worcester and then to Nicholas Arnold in 1627. It was then altered to give its façade a classical symmetry. A flight of steps leads from the terrace to a relocated central doorway, behind which the screens passage was removed and the old Great Hall turned into an entrance hall. A rear extension and new staircase were added. The Arnolds were fierce and intolerant Protestants and their fortunes ebbed and flowed with the religious feuds of their times, eventually ebbing. The house passed through various (mostly English) hands, including Mr Edward Bennett who bought it in 1924. He removed much Edwardian fenestration, including a giant oriel window, reinstating the original Jacobean appearance. In 1945 the house was acquired by Somerset Hopkinson, a descendant of the earlier owners, the Earls of Worcester. His descendants own it to this day.

The interior is remarkably of a piece, that of a 17th-century manorial residence in which original and restored features are in harmony. Whether the ceiling plasterwork in the hall is old or a replica, or the beams, or the panelling, or the dresser, seems immaterial. Ghosts of the medieval house linger

Above The Queen's Room on the first floor at Llanvihangel is so called because Elizabeth I is said to have slept here. The window to the left of the fireplace looks out onto the main staircase; it was blocked until opened up again in recent restoration. Below The impressive main staircase is made of yew and lit by modern stained-glass windows, the work of Dudley Forsyth; one depicts Charles I and his family, the other shows Queen Elizabeth I and Sir Walter Raleigh.

in such features as the step of the old hall dais and the holly and ebony frieze in the morning room.

The staircase, entirely of yew, rises through the entire house to the attic and is so grand it might have been imported from elsewhere. Hound gates guard the upstairs rooms from animal intrusion. Modern stained glass depicts supposed visits to Llanvihangel by Elizabeth I and Charles I.

The stair landing gives access to what would have been the old great chamber above the hall. Its splendid doorcase reflects this status. The chamber is now the Queen's Room, from Elizabeth's putative presence. The plaster ceiling is of intertwined Tudor roses and fleur-de-lis. Opposite is the King's Room (for Charles). All chambers are richly beamed and some contain linenfold panelling. In the kitchen is a charcoal precursor of an Aga dated 1679.

Llanvihangel still has stables built by the Arnolds for their breeding horses. They retain their original 17th-century stalls with handsome turned posts. Such survivals are rare in England, and can be seen at Little Peover, Cheshire, but unique in Wales.

Raglan castle

★★☆ Ostentatious late-medieval castle with moated Grand Tower

Near Raglan, 6 miles SW of Monmouth; Cadw, open all year

Raglan ranks with Chepstow as a majestic fortress of the southern Marches, yet it is an oddity among Welsh castles. It dates neither from the Norman era nor from the rebellions of the Llywelyns or Glyndwr. It was built later in the mid-15th century when Wales was more or less at peace, and by a Welsh adventurer, Sir William ap Thomas, the 'blue knight of Gwent'. He founded the great Welsh dynasty of the Herberts and lies in effigy in Abergavenny church with his wife, Gwladus. He had done well fighting the French and returned to build himself a Welsh Bodiam, a castle as much for show as for defence.

He began the Great Tower on the model of a French citadel in 1434. Building continued under his son, who became 1st Earl of Pembroke, and under successive members of that family, halting only briefly with the beheading of Pembroke, a Yorkist, in 1469 during the brief Lancastrian revival. Raglan then passed by marriage in 1508 to the ubiquitous Somersets, Earls of Worcester and cousins of Henry Tudor. They converted the domestic ranges into a full Tudor palace, as at Carew and Laugharne.

A little-known feature of the Tudor era in Wales is that its leading figures had shared exile with Henry Tudor on the Continent, returning after Bosworth in 1485 steeped in the culture of Europe's most developed Renaissance courts in Burgundy and the Low Countries. A similar injection of French and Dutch taste occurred with the return of the Stuarts after the Commonwealth in the 1660s.

In its prime in the early 16th century, Raglan was one of the great Renaissance houses of Britain. Its approach, through a gate flanked by prominent hexagonal towers, was apparently modelled on the Duke of Orleans' chateau at Aisne. The Great Hall and ceremonial chambers were adorned with

tapestries and Flemish manuscript books. The scale of entertainment was lavish. Wales under Henry VII was awakening from a long sleep.

Little of this period survives, apart from architectural fragments of the hall and long gallery. In the 17th century, with the Marches at peace and the Royalist Worcesters becoming Dukes of Beaufort, the castle was abandoned and its fittings and its glory moved to the family's more accessible seat of Badminton. The great parlour chimneypiece at Badminton is said to come from Raglan, which is still owned by the Beauforts.

The castle was later re-fashioned to the requirements of the Regency picturesque. Ivy grew and covered the wounds of age. Ghosts flirted with owls in the turrets and crumbling windows. The 20th century brought 'stabilization' and Raglan now sits immaculate amid lawns. The dramatically leaning slice of the slighted Great Tower looks like the design for an opera set.

The approach to the castle remains impressive, with the gatehouse, flared machicolations and Great Tower forming a composition visible from a distance and unlike any other in Wales. This is no gaunt Norman keep but the citadel of a grandee in the Marcher tradition but more intent on impressing than suppressing the surrounding populace.

The moated Great Tower to the left is the earliest part of the castle, built by Rhys ap Thomas as a self-contained residential stronghold surrounded by water and reached by a bridge. Its slighted wall tilts alarmingly – or now picturesquely – outwards, revealing hanging fireplaces and window frames.

The main gatehouse leads into Pitched Stone Court, so named after its cobbled surface. Large fireplaces survive in the Kitchen Tower, while the buttery range leads to the Great Hall. This has a spacious oriel window and the arms of the Earls of Worcester over the dais and would once have been a scene of great magnificence.

Beyond lies the Fountain Court and the private family chambers, including a chapel and long gallery with views north-west towards the Brecon Beacons. Immediately below the Fountain Court wall remain buried some of the most remarkable Renaissance terraces and water gardens in Britain. We await their reinstatement.

Above Gargoyles can still be seen on Raglan's gatehouse. **Right** In one corner of the Fountain Court stand the remains of the 15th-century porch. This led to the grand stairs which in turn led to the residential apartments.

112

Tredegar house

★★★☆ The greatest of Wales's Restoration mansions

2 miles SW Newport; private house, open part year

The house of the Morgans at Tredegar is equal only to Powys among the great houses of Wales. The land was owned by the same family from the 14th century to the 20th. A substantial medieval house on the site was first rebuilt as a result of John ap Morgan's support for Henry Tudor at Bosworth and was grand enough to receive Charles I after Naseby in 1645. Some of this house survives behind the new house built at the Restoration.

Rebuilding began *c*1670 with the judicious marriage of a Royalist Morgan, who had joined the Stuart court in Continental exile, to the daughter of a wealthy lawyer. The Dutch style was much admired by returning exiles. Tredegar is, says Newman in *Pevsner*, 'one of the outstanding houses of the Restoration period in the whole of Britain ... a great statement of dynastic wealth and self-confidence.' The architect is unknown but is believed to have been two Warwickshire brothers named Hurlbutt.

The house survived into the 18th century when it passed through the female line to the entrepreneur, Sir Charles Gould, who changed his name to Gould Morgan. Like the Butes of Cardiff and the Talbots of Margam, Morgan (1726–1806) capitalized on the growth of industrial south

Wales. A tramway through the park was nicknamed 'the golden mile' for the tolls charged on vehicles using it to reach the docks. A later Morgan took part in the Charge of the Light Brigade, an incident commemorated in a monument to his horse, Sir Brigg, in the garden to the east of the house. In 1859 the Morgans became Barons Tredegar.

The one thing the family did not do, unlike many of their contemporaries, was apply their new wealth to rebuilding their ancestral home. A modest Victorian reordering of the interior moved the entrance from one Restoration range to the other, but any changes had to be approved by the 1st Baron Tredegar's brother, Octavius Morgan, an antiquarian and ardent enthusiast for 17th-century architecture.

The Lords of Tredegar limped on into the 1930s when Evan Tredegar entertained Charlie Chaplin, Nancy Cunard and Evelyn Waugh, together with a menagerie of assorted parrots and boxing kangaroos. His extravagance followed by three bouts of death duties led the last of the Morgans to sell the house in 1951 and flee to the casinos of Monte Carlo.

After the family's departure, Tredegar entered the familiar purgatory. It was a school for 23 years and was then sold to Newport council, under whose inadequate charge it was described in the 1977 Companion Guide as 'in a kind of limbo, with vandals smashing everything they can lay their hands on'. A programme of restoration ensued and Newport eventually redeemed itself. The house is now superbly repaired, furnished and displayed.

Key to understanding the exterior is that there are two remarkably similar façades at right angles to each other, both enriched. The original intention was to build four ranges, but money ran out and the two lesser sides of the internal court survive from the pre-Restoration house. This gives Tredegar a pleasing sense of evolving over time. The main façade (on the far side of

the present entrance) is guarded by iron gates made by William Edney in 1714. The 11 bays are of two storeys plus an attic with a hipped roof, a customary Restoration composition. The roof was altered and a central lantern removed under the Regency, to give it a lower and perhaps more fashionable pitch. It still seems perfectly in balance.

The windows are unusually adorned with broken pediments surmounted by a lion and a gryphon, supporters of the Morgan arms. The effect is of a sculpted garland thrown round the entire exterior. The front door is similarly decorated with Italianate barley-sugar columns, emblems of Royalist sympathy. To the left is the secondary façade of nine bays with similarly enriched windows. The two façades, both of which have doors that serve as entrances, are easily confused.

The interior is astonishing not just for its decoration but for remaining largely as it would have appeared in the 17th century, thanks to the care shown in its Victorian restoration by Octavius Morgan. The new side entrance hall is in dark wood with family portraits and a seated statue of Sir Charles Morgan (1760–1846). Off one side is the morning room, furnished as a ladies' sitting room, and off the other is the dining room. Here the panelling is original, though the ceiling is a Victorian re-creation. The windows contain armorial stained glass and the dinner service is in the family colours of blue and gold. A secret panel leads to the kitchen.

The former entrance hall, or 'new hall' to distinguish it from that in the old Tudor house, has its original panelling. The two other ground floor rooms are Tredegar's stars. The Brown Room retains its 1680s panelling, alive with deeply undercut foliage on panels, pilasters, roundels, swags and bolection mouldings. The doors are crowned with scroll pediments filled with classical busts. They include the emperor Augustus and his wife Livia, perfectly at home in

Right The magnificent ceiling of the Gilt Room was copied from an engraving of Pietro da Cortona's painting, *The Glorification of Pope Urban VIII's Reign*, from the Palazzo Barberini in Rome. In this allegorical work, the figure of Wisdom, a representation of the Pope, overcomes Lust, portrayed as a naked woman, and Intemperance, represented by Silenus.

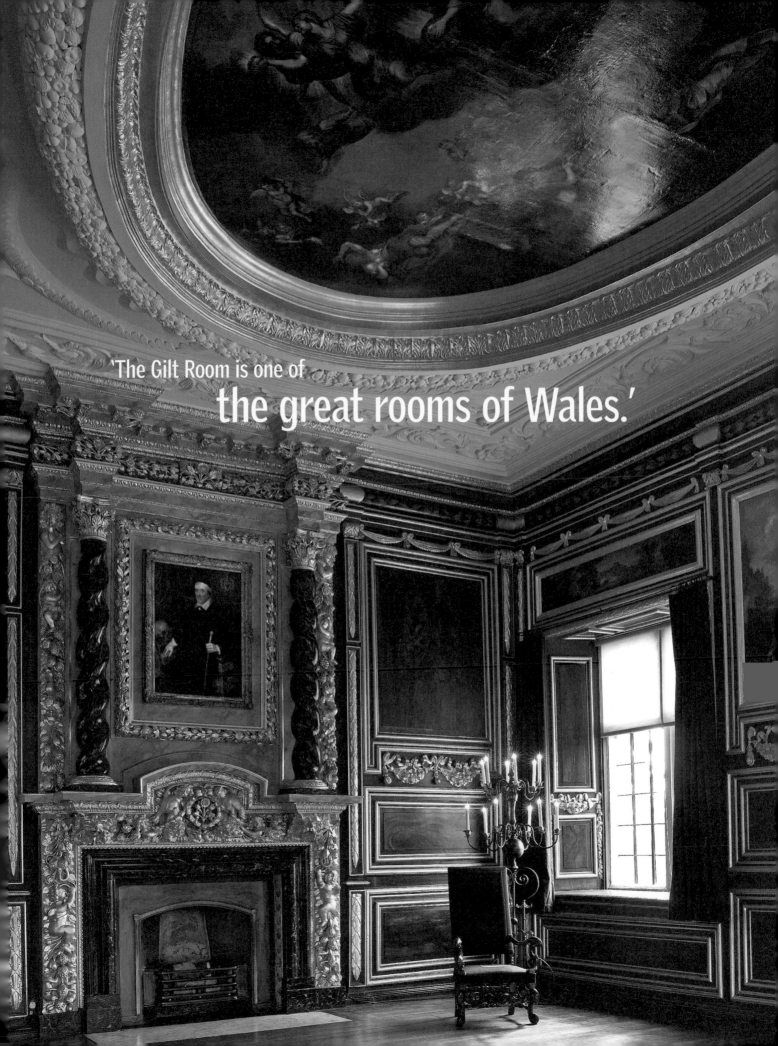

'The Gilt Room is one of
the great rooms of Wales.'

Above The elaborate oak carving of the Brown Room was probably completed in the 1680s, when the room was in use as the State Dining Room. A painted plaster bust of Livia is set above one of the doors, supported by carvings of musical instruments; a bust of her husband, the Emperor Augustus, stands above the other doorway in the room.

Restoration Gwent. The Gilt Room is one of the great rooms of Wales. The ceiling surrounds a painting copied from the Palazzo Barberini, illustrating Pope Urban's glorification of Rome by his improbable conquest of Lust and Intemperance. The chimneypiece and overmantel drips with gilding and frames a picture of William Morgan, *c*1650, whose grandson built the new house. Barley-sugar columns salute fat cherubs climbing swags heavy with fruit. The walls are covered in paintings built into the panelling, grained to look like walnut. The panels are adorned with swags and drops.

The sumptuousness continues upstairs with bedrooms and dressing rooms appropriate to various stages in the house's history, including Evan Tredegar's dabbling in the occult. The service wing has been restored in all its particulars, down to the jars of spice in the housekeeper's room.

Treowen

★ ★ Isolated Jacobean mansion, carefully restored

At Wonastow, 3 miles SW of Monmouth; private house, open part year

North Monmouthshire turns its back on the world and loses itself in the foothills of the Beacons. Along the road from Jingle Street is the tiny hamlet of Wonastow, from where a lane leads north into a wilderness of dark woods and tumbling contours. Suddenly an old Jacobean pile comes into view on top of a hill, with no sign of other habitation.

The house had been in the same family since its construction in the early 17th century. Then, in 1954, it was sold to the present owners, the Wheelocks. It has been carefully restored, if sparsely furnished, and is let out for weekends and marriage parties. I can imagine no wilder spot from which to set out on the journey of matrimony.

The exterior is austere for 1627, when it was built for a family named Jones on a grand scale; a doubled pile with façades front and back. Only a later front porch is enriched, with two tiers of doubled columns, crowned by a coat of arms in the pediment. For some reason the top storey of this range was removed in the 18th century, giving the side elevations a lopsided look. The stone mullioned windows are regular and severe. When the front was a full three storeys, the house must have looked like a fortress.

The interior has been much altered, but the beautifully composed classical screen was restored in 2001. The ground floor, apart from the hall, is mostly kitchens and services. The chief feature of the house is one of the most spectacular staircases of any house of this period. It fills an open stairwell the entire three storeys to the attic. Even the servants were beneficiaries of the owner's ostentation. The work is crafted of turned newel posts with pendants and finials. The view up from below is breathtaking.

On the first floor the old Great Chamber survives, with what appears to be its original frieze and plasterwork ceiling. The present owners are trying to reinstate as much as they can of the original fittings and acquire maps and portraits of the estate. It is a valiant endeavour.

Usk castle

★ ★ Norman castle, now picturesque ruins

At Usk, 10 miles SW of Monmouth; private house, open all year

Usk Castle is privately owned and everything a Cadw castle is not. It is wild, unmanicured and idiosyncratic. Vegetation is everywhere. Where a government castle is scrubbed and tidy, Usk respects the dishevelment of age. The car park is lost in the woods.

The approach is past the owner's family home, fashioned from the medieval gatehouse (c1375), and the stables still have horses. The outer ward of the castle is now the garden of the house, with paddock and herbaceous border. Visitors are asked to put a pebble in a basket ('we are told we must count numbers') and entrance money in a dish, the most casual and economical unmanned entry control I know.

The castle was built by the de Clares during their sovereignty of the southern Marches in the 12th century. The walled inner ward is reached up a path strewn with fuchsia and Virginia creeper and past the foot of a massive Norman keep of 1170. This was built by the Norman warlord, Richard 'Strongbow' de Clare, and the castle took on its present form under the equally ferocious William Marshal, who won de Clare's daughter for unseating the future Richard I in a joust in 1189.

Marshal added his distinctive innovation, a round 'garrison' tower, at the time of the castle's fortification against Llywelyn the Great in the 13th century. It then passed to the Mortimers and, in the 18th century, the Beauforts. It has been in private ownership ever since.

The pleasure of Usk lies in the present rather than the past. If ruins must be ruins, let them be like this, as if playing a game with the surrounding rocks and enveloping vegetation. The centre of the ward is rough grass with roses and creeper clinging to the walls. Round the perimeter are the remains of turrets, a chapel and the Great Hall. Marshal's garrison tower rises four storeys. More recent features include geese and a yew peacock. The treasure tower, still inhabited, was once occupied by 'a dog called coker', believed to be the first reference to a cocker spaniel.

White castle

★★☆ Lonely fortress with spectacular views

8 miles E of Abergavenny; Cadw, open all year

White is my favourite among the castles of the Marches. It is both the wildest and the most complete, with sensational views over the Usk valley to the Brecon Beacons. The original Norman fortress was substantially altered in the mid-13th century against Llywelyn ap Gruffudd but there was no adjacent village or church. The castle appears to have been abandoned by the 16th century, sparing it Civil War slighting. The name comes from its old lime wash, sadly vanished.

The outer ward is a spacious parade ground, now grassy, surrounded by a dry ditch, wall and towers. To the left the main castle and inner ward rises across a deep moat, a remarkable engineering feat on top of a hill. The castle walls rise on a steep mound and from below look wholly impregnable. The gatehouse across what would have been a drawbridge is massive, flanked by drum towers from which can be enjoyed a 360-degree view. From here south Wales might be a deserted landscape, composed only of woods, fields and mountains.

'... my favourite among the castles of the Marches.'

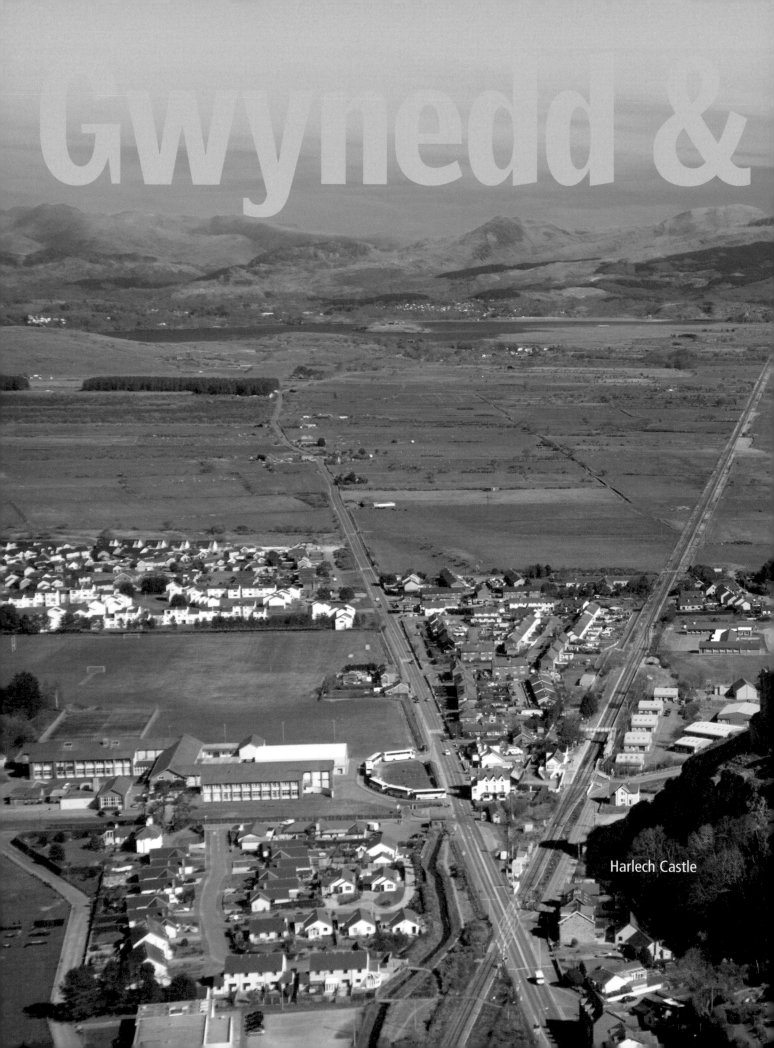

Gwynedd &

Harlech Castle

Anglesey

Gwynedd & Anglesey

Beaumaris castle

★ ★ ★ Medieval fortress-palace, Edward I's intended headquarters in Anglesey

Castle Street, Beaumaris; Cadw, open all year

The town of Beaumaris is little adulterated by modern development and has surely the loveliest location in Wales, looking out over the Menai Straits with Snowdonia for a backdrop. It was founded by Edward I after the death of Llywelyn and became the centre of his administration and later the county town of Anglesey. Named 'beautiful marsh' (from the same root at Paris's Marais) to attract sceptical Norman settlers, it has the atmosphere of a Kent cinque port. A handsome high

BEAUMARIS

street is lined with coaching inns and houses used by island gentry during the assize. The county courthouse and prison survive, restored and open to the public. The moated castle is cosily located at one end of the street.

Beaumaris Castle is no great fortress. It is the undamaged, though unfinished, climax to the great works undertaken in Wales by Edward I's master-builder, Master James of St George. Like Bodiam in Sussex, everything suggests a building for comfort and show rather than defence. This was to be a secure headquarters of the English occupation of the Principality, to accommodate the king and his retinue of soldiers, judges and administrators. Suites of rooms were to be constructed here, protected not from a main force but from native insurgency.

The castle was begun in 1295, the inhabitants of the former Welsh town of Llanfaes being moved to the duly named Newborough. Though devoid of natural advantages, the site shows James of St George at his most sophisticated, with concentric rings of a moat, supplied from the sea, an outer wall, an outer ward and a massive inner wall. Attackers entering by the sea gate had to run the gauntlet of a barbican and a south gate with ten obstacles. They need have no fear today. In a display of Welsh contempt for English occupation, a children's playground has been defiantly sited in place of the seaward moat. The effect is from some angles to reduce Beaumaris to a doll's house.

The walls are of a deep russet sandstone with occasional white chequerboarding. The inner ward is spacious and has the appearance more of a fortified palace than a castle. The walls bear the relics of old fireplaces, while on the far side, in the northern gatehouse, were to be domestic apartments. This gatehouse palace was a feature of St George's plans – there is another at Harlech. Here it was never completed. Five great windows look down on the ward, with an upper stage unbuilt.

The castle walls are a maze of passages, sleeping chambers and latrines, the mod cons of a medieval fortress. Inside one of the towers is a charming small chapel built of limestone with polygonal apse, graceful ribbing and trefoil arcading. Thoroughly restored it makes one long for similar restoration elsewhere on the site.

The Old Gaol

★★★ Victorian gaol and model of prison reform

Steeple Street, Beaumaris; museum, open part year

Occupying a complete block in the old town, the walls of Beaumaris gaol rise impressively over the surrounding streets, far more terrifying than the castle. This was the prison not just for the borough but for the whole island and was the result of Robert Peel's 1823 Gaol Act, laying down conditions that would be considered spacious in a prison today.

Previous prisons had been mostly medieval in every sense, corrupt in their management, their cells rat-infested and prisoners manacled to prevent escape. Among other improvements, the inmates were now weighed on admission and discharge to ensure they had been well fed, and given work and wages. Exact quantities of food and clothing were stipulated, for men and women separately. The design of the building was by a Yorkshireman, Hansom, of cab fame and included a separate 'house of correction' for

BEAUMARIS

'... far more terrifying than the castle.'

lesser offenders such as vagrants. When prisons were taken over by the Home Office in 1877, Beaumaris had fewer than a dozen prisoners, who were sent to Caernarfon. The gaol became a police station and lockup.

Today it is kept as on the day it closed, demonstrating a Victorian revolution in social reform, treating humans with a measure of dignity. The community clearly tried to help transgressors to rehabilitate themselves in the context of the town. In this it appears less soul destroying than any modern equivalent.

The prison is of 40 rooms on two floors, shaped as a T with exercise and work yards at the back. There was a gibbet for public hangings, so they could be seen from the street. The condemned cell was twice the size of ordinary ones and had its own fireplace. That said, only two executions ever took place, one of a man bitterly protesting his innocence. He cursed the church clock opposite, which is said never to have kept the right time since.

Other facilities include a chapel with a fireplace and admonitory verses on the walls, reminding inmates of the justice of God (though not His forgiveness), an infirmary, laundry, washroom, kitchen, women's workroom and connecting nursery. At the rear is the only treadmill left in a British prison. The users worked a water pump, ten minutes on and ten minutes off for eight hours. As a result, all cells had running water, a luxury beyond the experience of most people outside.

Left A new wing was added in 1867, but the prison was closed within ten years. **Above right** The condemned cell was larger than normal cells, with a solid bed rather than the typical hammock.
Right The gaol had its own laundry where women inmates washed clothing and other linens.

Bodysgallen hall

⭐ Jacobean mansion built around a medieval tower house

2 miles S of Llandudno; now a hotel

The old medieval-cum-Jacobean hall of the prominent Mostyn family is now a luxury hotel, proud of its past and careful of its present. The core of the building is an old tower house, similar to the pele towers of the Scottish borders. This was probably built in the late 13th century as a watchtower for Conwy castle, located in the tumbling hills of Pydew behind Llandudno. Here we must imagine Norman soldiers far from home manning its roof-top and signalling to Conwy of an approaching Welsh horde. There is a fine view (accessible on polite request).

The property passed by marriage from the Mostyns to the no less ubiquitous Wynns. It was Robert Wynn who built the present house *c*1620, essentially medieval in form, with a hall on the ground floor (now the reception area) and Great Chamber above (now the drawing room). Both have overmantels with extrovert heraldry, depicting the Wynn and Mostyn pedigrees, similar to those in the Wynns' Plas Mawr (see page 135). A later Wynn married back into the Mostyns in the 18th century.

The Victorians took Bodysgallen in hand in the 1890s, adding a new dining room and a neo-Jacobean staircase enclosing the ancient tower, as at another former Mostyn property, Gloddeath Hall, across the valley. Most remarkable was the restoration of the 17th-century garden, which appears not to have suffered from Regency romanticization and whose terraces and walks have been well-restored by the hotel's owner, Richard Broyd.

Bryn Bras castle

Right The sitting room in the flag tower at Bryn Bras is circular in shape. Norman-style blind arcading runs around the walls of the room, interrupted by a row of windows set in similar arches and a curved door. The zigzag patterning on the doorway and cornice, as well as other architectural motifs, are typically found in surviving Norman buildings, such as Durham Castle.

 Regency neo-Norman mansion

4½ miles E of Caernarfon; private house, open by arrangement

The owner of Bryn Bras was appalled to hear that I had come hotfoot from mighty Penrhyn. I should have seen his first, he said. Bryn Bras was the work of Penrhyn's creator, Thomas Hopper, apparently a sketch in the margin of the great castle. It is more than a doodle, rather a rare neo-Norman country house displaying all Hopper's dexterity.

Bryn Bras is owned and lived in by Mr and Mrs Gray-Parry, with some holiday apartments available for rent. Originally a farm it was converted in the 1820s for Thomas Williams into a towered keep and residence. This has four turrets, rising two storeys above an arcade of wide Norman arches. The house is beautifully set in 30 acres of ornamental gardens on a knoll overlooking the meadows towards Caernarfon and Anglesey.

The interior is stately but not grand. A Norman doorway gives onto a hall alive with patterned decoration, dark and lit with coloured decorative glass. Steps to the left rise to a round flag tower, whose two circular chambers are filled with Hopper's favourite motifs, intersecting blind arcading and zigzags. The heads of the arches are all different and even the door is curved. The upper room has a slate fireplace.

In the main body of the house, the drawing room, dining room and sitting room are more sparing in their Norman. One has an Art-Nouveau frieze beneath a Norman cornice. On the stairs a 20th-century owner, Duncan Alves, inserted heraldic stained glass on the basis of a promised knighthood that never arrived.

The library is a workaday room but with a surprise, an arched window bay in the form of a Catholic chapel, adorned with three windows depicting faith, hope and charity. It was used when the house was a school during the war and former girls still return to gaze on the revered spot.

Caernarfon castle

★★★★☆ Strategic fortress and royal palace, one of the great castles of Wales

At Caernarfon, 8 miles SW of Bangor; Cadw, open all year

Caernarfon, fortress, palace and emblem of alien rule 'is one of the most striking buildings the middle ages have left to us,' or so claims the guidebook with some justice. Legend holds that Constantine the Great, first Christian emperor of Rome in the 4th century AD, was born here to the wife of a Welsh noble, Macsen Wledig. Later in life the emperor is said to have dreamt of a castle at the mouth of a fair river among high mountains, its turrets crowned with golden Roman eagles.

The site was indeed a Roman colony and the town's mother church is on the old Roman camp outside the town at Llanbeblig. The Normans recognized the strategic value of the location and built a motte and bailey on the present castle promontory. Gwynedd princes lived here through the 12th and 13th centuries, including Llywelyn the Great: it was the final suppression of his grandson's revolt in 1282 that led to Edward I's colossal rebuilding.

Caernarfon was the greatest of the fortifications begun that year by the king's builder, Master James of St George. It was intended to evoke the spirit of Welsh history, the Roman occupation and the walls of Constantinople, a European display of kingship. Into its walls were built bands of red sandstone imitating bands on the walls of Constantinople.

When Edward and Queen Eleanor arrived from Conwy in July 1283 they stayed in timber apartments, but when they returned the following Easter the Eagle Tower was sufficiently habitable,

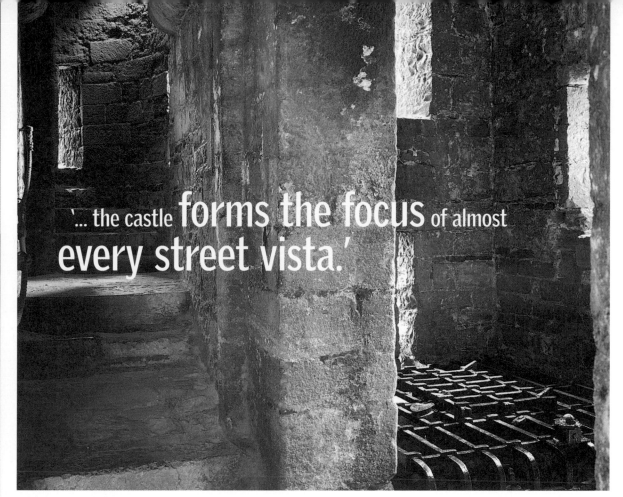

'... the castle **forms the focus** of almost **every street vista.**'

Above On the ground-floor of the Well Tower the original well-shaft can still be seen, now covered with a metal grille. Almost 50 feet deep, the well-shaft could also be accessed from the first floor above. A lead-lined cistern next to the well-head was linked to the kitchen by lead pipes running through the walls and would have been kept full of water.

so it was said, to see the birth of the future Prince of Wales, Edward. Both the castle and the town walls were complete within five years and accounts for fitting out cease after 1292. The outlay was a vast sum for the time, £12,000.

Despite this expense, Caernarfon proved vulnerable to Welsh insurgency. In 1294 Madog ap Llywelyn's forces overwhelmed the castle and town and burned anything that could be destroyed. Edward promptly ordered the castle repaired and strengthened, a task continuing until 1304. Turrets were added to the Eagle Tower and Llywelyn's Great Hall was brought from Conwy and re-erected in the inner ward.

Caernarfon remained a closed English settlement for two centuries and Edward's reinforcement enabled it to withstand Glyndwr's rebellion with just 28 armed men in 1403–4. After 1485 the Tudor ascendancy reduced the need for such bastions of English power and the buildings fell into decay. Only the Eagle Tower was re-roofed in 1620. The castle was garrisoned by Royalists during the Civil War but not seriously damaged afterwards, despite orders for its slighting. Caernarfon was thus able to survive into the picturesque age externally intact. A late Victorian deputy-constable restored it with a vigour that would be deplored today, but prevented further ruination. It saw investitures of Princes of Wales in 1911 and, amid much-ridiculed solemnity, in 1969.

In the 20th century the castle suffered its most ignominious assault, from a car park directly under its south wall. This ruined the view of its walls rising from the River Seiont, as painted by Turner and Wilson. The zigzag wall with its towers and battlements is made to look like a film backdrop. The approach from the town is more impressive, where the castle forms the focus of almost every street vista.

The interior is set round two great wards or courts, one leading out of the other and defined by five towers. The entrance is through the King's Gate, as fiercely defended as that at Beaumaris. The guide offers half a dozen ways in which a hostile visitor might be painfully eliminated. The gate included a chapel and potentially a hall, never completed. On the exterior is an eroded but original (1321) statue of Edward II, first Prince of Wales.

Most of the interior of the castle now has the familiar form of 'ruins in a lawn', round which visitors tend to wander in a daze. Understanding what each block of stone, arch or dank chamber once meant is left to the imagination. The Eagle Tower was supposedly the fortified palace of whoever represented the king in Wales, initially the lieutenant, Sir Otto de Grandison. Three storeys of grand chambers have smaller rooms off them in turrets, including latrines. They are now used for exhibitions and other museology. There is still an excellent view from the battlements.

The Queen's and Chamberlain towers contain a regimental museum, with between them the footings of the old Great Hall, centre of hospitality for the English settlement. The remaining towers are composed of passages and chambers, chiefly for defence. The upper ward of the castle was completed only in part and much was restored in the 19th century.

Below The Eagle Tower, topped with three individual turrets, was the finest of Caernarfon's towers. The battlements of both tower and turrets were originally decorated with figures carved from stone – the remains of a much-weathered eagle still look out from the western-most of the turrets.

Cochwillan Old hall

★ Medieval freestanding hall, now restored as a drawing room

Near Llanrug, 4 miles E of Caernarfon; private house, open by arrangement

Right The hammerbeam ceiling at Cochwillan is more than 30 feet long, divided into three bays. At the eastern end of the hall the room has been extended a further half-bay by moving the timbered wall back; this also allows the gothic window at the dais end to be fully appreciated.

Cochwillan is the freestanding hall of a medieval courtyard house, built in the 1450s for William ap Gruffydd. He was a supporter of Henry Tudor at Bosworth and rewarded as Sheriff of Caernarfon for life. The hall fell into ruin after being abandoned in 1870 but was restored in 1970 by the Penrhyn estate as the drawing room of an adjacent private house. It is used for charity events and is open by appointment.

The hall is a superb relic of its period. The approach is from what would have been the outside of the old courtyard, the original entrance being from within. The dais end is thus to the left of the present door and the great fireplace is on the present entrance side. Restoration moved back a timbered wall, which had been partitioned for extra accommodation, to allow the Perpendicular window to serve its original purpose of lighting the dais. The other windows are simple trefoils.

The roof is a hammerbeam construction with shields on the terminals. The timbers are dressed with chamfering and there is an intricate carved frieze, all signs of prosperous ownership. The room is furnished for contemporary living, with sofas, heaters, shelves and clutter. While it cannot always be warm – the owner's most reliable heating system, she says, is a trampoline – Cochwillan shows that any historic building can serve a use.

CONWY

Conwy castle

★★★★☆ One of Edward I's magnificent castles with intact outer walls

Rose Hill Street, Conwy; Cadw, open all year

Conwy is another of Edward I's fortresses, masculine to Caernarfon's feminine. Both have suffered grievous assault, not from war but from subsequent engineering. In Conwy's case the offence is near unbelievable, not one but three bridges driven over the river head-on to its walls, veering to either side at the last minute to leave the castle marooned as if on a motorway roundabout. Since pictures of the castle cannot avoid featuring these bridges they have become part of the castle composition.

Conwy, with its backdrop of hills, streets and quayside, is the most spectacular of Edward I's boroughs. Thomas Telford's box girder bridge (1848) at least deferred to it in erecting castellated gateways at each end, while the adjacent footbridge has embattled suspension towers. The 1950s road bridge – rendered superfluous by a 1991 tunnel – should be removed and an attempt made to recapture Turner's 'sublime and overwhelming emotion' on seeing and painting the castle in 1798.

The castle was begun at the same time as Caernarfon in 1283 and took ten years to complete. The builder was again Master James of St George, assisted on site by Richard of Chester, using as the base a bare rock surrounded by water and marsh. The castle remains intact to outward view, its walls and eight fortified towers undamaged, as are the 21 towers that line the town's walls. Turrets, passageways, windows, arrow slits and battlements are all in good repair. The 'slighting' of one wall during the Commonwealth was, ironically, rectified by the railway company when driving its track past the gap. Conwy is one of the great achievements of medieval military architecture in Europe.

'... one of **the great** achievements of military **medieval architecture** ...'

Right The royal apartments at Conwy included a small chapel in the Chapel Tower, where the king and queen could look down on services from a private 'watching chamber' above.

The interior has none of Caernarfon's lax spaciousness though St George divided it similarly into inner and outer wards. The outer ward, the first approached from the entrance, contains the curved outline of the Great Hall partitioned by arches, only one of which survives. The towers were used as barracks, kitchens and a prison. A middle gate in a separate wall leads to the inner ward where were the royal apartments.

These survive, albeit roofless, built into the castle wall, with bedrooms and a great chamber for receiving guests. They were occupied only twice, by Edward himself on his return to Wales in 1295 and by Richard II before disastrously confronting Bolingbroke at Flint in 1399. Though they appear bleak and the windows have lost their tracery, they are rare examples of fortress accommodation of this period. There is a small vaulted chapel in the Chapel Tower, with lovely lancet windows.

Aberconwy house

 ✶✶ The townhouse of a medieval merchant

Castle Street, Conwy; National Trust, open part year

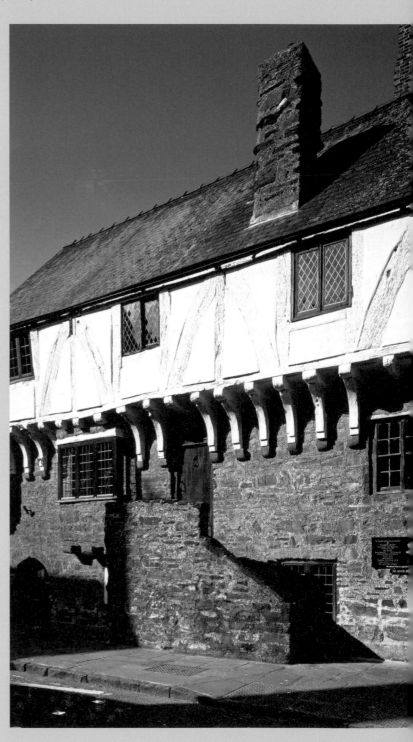

Aberconwy House is a surviving medieval merchant's house of a type that all but vanished for post-war street widening. The house was built in the mid-16th century, though parts date from the 13th. The latter may be the work of English masons travelling in Edward I's retinue.

The house has a stone-walled ground floor with basement, above which rises a timber-framed upper floor – true 'half-timbering'. The occupants were initially merchants but later included a coffee shop, temperance hotel, museum and antiques shop. When threatened with removal to America, where these buildings were more appreciated, the house was bought and donated to the National Trust in 1934.

The ground floor is reached by an external staircase so distinctive that one resident, Samuel Williams, was nicknamed 'Sam Pen y Grisiau' or Sam Top-of-Stairs. The downstairs comprises just two rooms, a kitchen and living room. The former carries robust carpentry in the form of two magnificent dressers with appropriate pewter, and a rare hanging bread crate to keep the bread away from vermin. The parlour is simply furnished in 18th-century style, which seems anachronistic.

Anachronistic too is a modern staircase inserted at the insistence of health and safety, spoiling the approach to the great chamber upstairs. This has now been partitioned into a living and bed room, the latter with 19th-century furniture. A storeroom contains a dreaded video screen.

Plas Mawr

★★★★ Significant Elizabethan townhouse of some splendour

High Street, Conwy; Cadw, open all year

The house of Robert Wynn, son of John Wynn of Gwydir, is the most splendid town mansion of the Tudor period remaining in Britain. Built in 1576, it shows the pride of the new Welsh mercantile class in being at last permitted to own property in an English settlement. The house is filled with motifs indicating Wynn's ancestry and commercial interests, as well as his loyalty to the Tudors. The initials RW occur everywhere.

Robert had served in the retinue of the British ambassador to Bruges and returned to Conwy at the age of 50, marrying Dorothy Griffith of Penrhyn and buying a plot of land to erect a new house within the town walls. After Robert's death the property was saved from destruction by being the subject of a long legal dispute. It was variously a school, a tenement and a business, partitioned, quartered and multi-occupied but never destroyed. Taken on by the Royal Cambrian Academy of Art in 1908, it featured in an early edition of *Country Life*.

The house exemplifies the European merchant house of the late Middle Ages. The street frontage was designed defensively

CONWY

and for business. The main house sits retiring beyond a courtyard surrounded by domestic offices. It has the traditional 16th-century plan of hall on the ground floor and Great Chamber on the first. However, the house was later expanded and its orientation turned to present an entrance front to the side street. This reorientation gives Plas Mawr much of its interest. The house is approached through its south wing with kitchens, pantries and brewhouse beyond. The entrance hall is airy with a vividly colourful overmantel of 1580, proclaiming the Wynns' princely ancestry to all visitors. It carries coats of arms, Tudor roses, pilasters and, most bizarre, bare-breasted caryatids with baskets of strawberries on their heads.

The ceilings and walls of most of the formal rooms are coated in swirling ribs into which are set heraldic and hunting motifs. The family parlour is downstairs among the domestic offices, on the site of what would have been the earlier hall. It carries the richest of plasterwork and must have been a warm and cosy retreat on a winter's day. Upstairs are three plastered rooms, two of them principal bedrooms with a servants' room between. These have been restored with their Jacobean furnishing.

Most spectacular is the Great Chamber, reached by two spiral staircases and overlooking the side street. The plasterwork here contains more family references and those of celebrated local worthies (who might have been entertained here). The overmantel celebrates Queen Elizabeth. The caryatids which line the walls look appropriately overawed. Ceiling bosses have been repainted and the floor laid with rush matting.

My only quarrel with Plas Mawr is that museologists have colonized every corner that is not part of the main suite of rooms. Visitors emerging from an Elizabethan environment are assailed with audio-visual displays, notice boards and computer screens. Atmosphere is replaced by education monotone. The red and white bedrooms are lost to this cause, as is the brewhouse. The attic, which should be a crammed, busy, squalid warren of stores and servants quarters, looks like something from a BBC makeover programme.

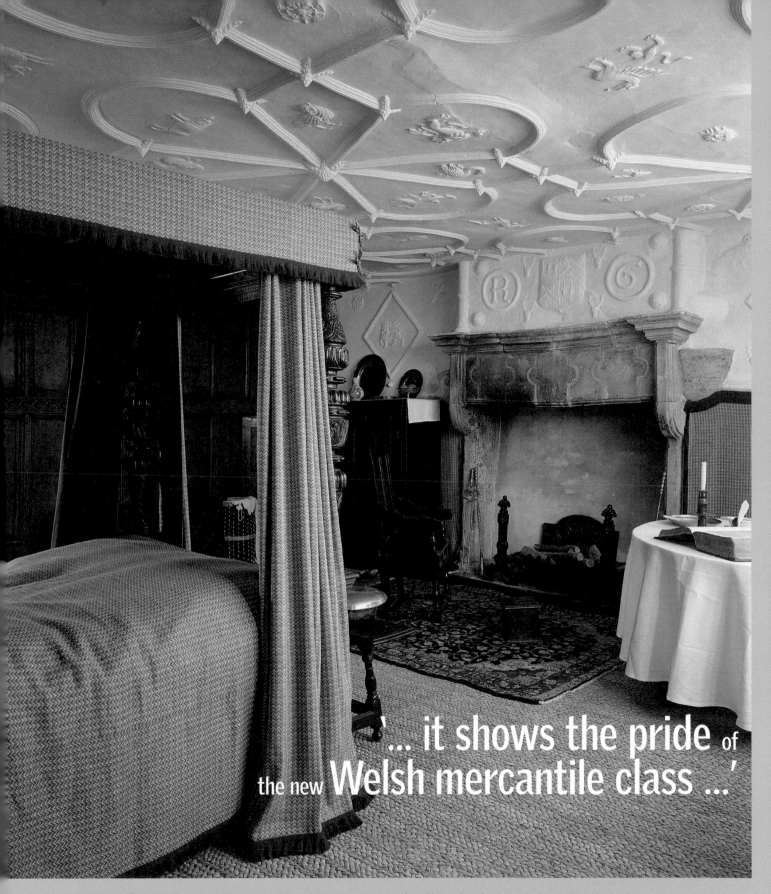

'... it shows the pride of the new **Welsh mercantile class** ...'

Above left The hall at Plas Mawr was where visitors were received and here the plasterwork decoration above the fireplace displays Robert Wynn's exalted ancestry. The family arms, at the centre of the overmantel, feature eagles and fleurs-de-lis, both emblems of the princes of Gwynedd. **Above** The same arms can be seen on the plasterwork overmantel of the 'chamber above the parlour', one of the two private family rooms on the first floor of the north range.

Din Lligwy

★★ Remains of a Romano-British village

Near Moelfre, 11 miles NW of Bangor; Cadw, open all year

This is the most evocative Romano-British settlement in Britain. Visitors must walk for half a mile across the fields before climbing to a clearing amid trees, immediately recognizable as an encampment. The place is thought to have been occupied in the late-Roman period, and presumably afterwards. Excavation has revealed 4th-century pottery and coins and evidence of ironworking.

The walls of two round huts and a number of rectangular ones survive, as do surrounding walls of considerable thickness. Since such villages would normally be of wood and daub, the scale of these buildings suggest a prosperous community. The walls rise waist high and door lintels are still standing.

With the trees dancing in the wind and a complete absence of modern buildings near the site the druidical past is made present. Here priests and bards incited their audience to remember their ancestors and reject the Christianizing wiles of Rome. Here Tacitus had the Romans determined to stamp out druidism, 'felling the groves dedicated to savage superstition', and thus ensuring their passage into Welsh myth.

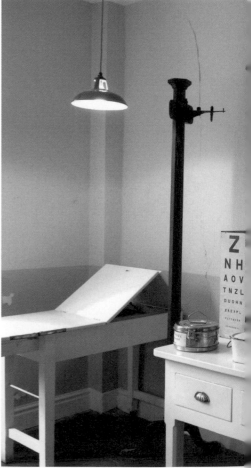

Dinorwic Quarry
hospital

⭐ Earliest industrial hospital, still equipped

Near Llanberis, 6 miles E of Caernarfon;
museum, open part year

Facing the north flank of Snowdon across Llanberis is the mighty gash of the Dinorwic slate quarry. Various schemes to landscape it have achieved little, leaving the works of man to return to nature of their own accord. A slate museum stands on the site of the old workshops, run by the National Museum of Wales. But the best impression of work in the quarries is gained by walking along the lake and up to a house built as a hospital for injured miners.

The building dates from 1840 and was an innovation in industrial medicine. There were some 3,000 miners at the time and accidents occurred daily. The hospital was supported by a small subscription taken from their wages. The treatment today looks primitive and mechanical, since the chief injuries were broken and crushed limbs, but the hospital remained in use into the 1950s, and continued to offer first aid for another ten years.

The original wards are in place, together with the dispensary, operating theatre, kitchen and the earliest X-ray machines to be used in Britain (1898). The terrace offers a magnificent view over Lake Padarn towards Snowdon.

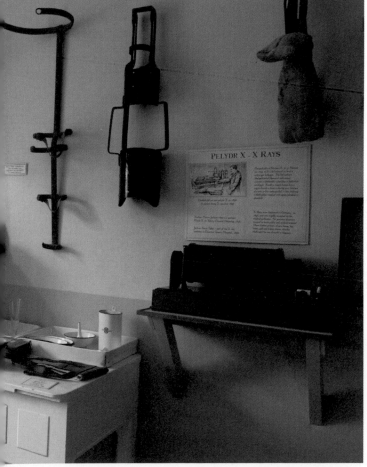

Left All manner of early medical equipment is preserved at the Quarry Hospital – the splints and braces bear witness to some of the most frequent injuries treated there. Many new treatments were pioneered at Dinorwic. The hospital was the first in Britain to acquire an X-ray machine, just over two years after German scientist Wilhelm Röntgen first demonstrated the technology by taking an X-ray picture of his wife's hand.

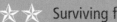 Surviving fortress of Llywelyn the Great on a wild mountain pass

Near Dolwyddelan, 6 miles SW of Betws-y-Coed; Cadw, open all year

Here is the best place in Gwynedd to sit and imagine the embattled princes of Wales retreating to defend their land from the invading English. Dolwyddelan is, like Castell y Bere and Criccieth, a Welsh castle built by the Welsh. The old keep stands high on the pass from Betws into the Ffestiniog valley under the shadow of Moel Siabod. On all sides rise bleak, untrammelled mountains, almost free of forestry and with little habitation in sight.

Dolwyddelan castle

'At Dolwyddelan **the view, and history, is all.'**

Dolwyddelan was built sometime after 1200 by Llywelyn the Great, though legend has him born in or near it in 1173. It was defended by his grandson, Llywelyn the Last, against Edward I but it fell in 1283, one of the last redoubts of independence in the principality.

The keep was supplemented by a curtain wall and, by the end of the 13th century, a second tower. This stands ruined on the far side of the courtyard. The castle was later acquired by Maredudd ap Ieuan, founder of the Tudor Wynn dynasty and a descendant of Llywelyn.

The keep is entered by steps to the original raised entrance, inside which is a roofed Great Chamber, with living quarters above. The upper stories date from the 15th century. There are no furnishings. At Dolwyddelan the view, and history, is all.

Llywelyn the Great
c1173–1240

The engraving above is taken from a 19th-century painting by George Cattermole, in which the artist imagined Llywelyn surrounded by his barons. Llywelyn ap Iorweth, who came to be known as Llywelyn Fawr, or Llywelyn the Great, was born c1173. By 1201 he had control over Gwynedd, the kingdom of his birth, and by 1218 he was the *de facto* ruler of Wales, having successfully unified his fellow Welsh nobleman against his father-in-law, and former ally, King John. Llywelyn maintained this authority throughout his lifetime and was also able to influence the Anglo-Norman rulers of the Welsh Marches by arranging the marriages of his children into important Marcher families.

Gwydir castle

★ ★ ★ Medieval mansion and historic seat on the banks of the Conwy

Near Llanwrst, 10 miles S of Conwy; private house, open part year

The story of the rescue of the Wynn seat of Gwydir is told in Judy Corbett's *Castles in the Air*, one of ceaseless struggle against adversity. Stripped of later accretions, the house has been returned to its medieval and later splendour by Corbett and her husband, Peter Welford. Cosily sited in a small park on the banks of the River Conwy, it is open to visitors and for bed and breakfast.

The house was the seat of Howel Coetmore, who served the Black Prince in France as commander of the celebrated Welsh bowmen. It was sold to Maredudd ap Ieuan of Dolwyddelan, who rebuilt the core of the present hall, and added the adjacent Tower. He died here in 1525 and is buried at Dolwyddelan church after fathering more than 30 children. His son John (d.1559) took the Anglicized surname of Wynn (the fair) and benefited from the dissolution of Maenan Abbey, fragments of which start like ghosts from the walls of Gwydir.

John was father of Robert Wynn of Plas Mawr (see page 135) in Conwy and grandfather of Sir John Wynn, late-Elizabethan landowner, businessman, scholar and politician. He extended Gwydir by building two ranges of outbuildings (now vanished) to form an enclosed courtyard. All that remains of this work is the splendid porch.

Gwydir, like many Welsh houses of its time, benefited from ceasing to be the chief residence of its proprietor and thus escaping demolition. It suffered an opposite fate in escaping repair. After this

'... the house has been **returned** to its **medieval and later splendour ...**'

Above In 1921 the 1640s panelling, fireplace, baroque doorcase and leatherwork frieze of Gwydir's dining room were sold to American newspaper magnate William Randolph Hearst. On his death in 1951 the pieces went to the Metropolitan Museum in New York. In 1996 Gwydir's new owners discovered them stored in a warehouse in the Bronx, and a happy home-coming was arranged.

branch of the Wynns died out in the 1670s, the house was owned by various English aristocrats until coming into the hands of the Victorian Marquis of Lincolnshire, under whom it saw a visit from the future George V and Queen Mary. It was sold in 1921 and disaster followed, the solar tower and west wing being gutted in separate fires. The place was abandoned until 1944 when it was bought by a well-meaning bank manager, Arthur Clegg.

While Clegg's renovation saved the building from certain ruin, its 'medievalization' damaged much of the original house. The superb 1640s panelling in the dining room had been sold in 1921 to William Randolph Hearst (see St Donat's, page 95) who bequeathed it to the Metropolitan Museum in New York. There it was discovered by the Welfords in its original packing cases, reacquired and brought back to Gwydir in 1998. The solar hall panelling, also sold in 1921, is still missing.

So complex is the architectural history of the house that a walk round it soon dissolves into detective work. Most confusing is that the old hall on the left of the courtyard, with the later 'hall of Maredudd' inserted above, was supplanted in importance by the solar tower, with its own first-floor Great Chamber. The old hall is earlier and moodily medieval, with rough stone walls, flagged floor and heavily-beamed ceiling. This would once have been open to the rafters and is a remarkable survival of a form altered beyond recognition in most houses of the period.

The hall of Maredudd was inserted around 1500 and is reached by a spiral staircase of *c*1540, encrusted with stone brought from Maenan Abbey, including gothic features in its top lantern. This

Left The hall of Maredudd commemorates Maredudd ap Ieuan (a name also sometimes seen written as Meredith ap Ifan), who became the owner of Gwydir in around 1490. The hall was one of his additions to the castle, inserted above the old hall in *c*1500.

hall has a wind-braced roof, gothic trefoil windows, two fireplaces and tapestries. Its screen is like the timber-framed outer wall of an old house, while behind is a massive fireplace that looks as if carved from the native rock and is awesomely vernacular.

To the east of these older halls are a garderobe tower and linking passage to the solar wing. Here is the solar reception room, still naked of its panelling, with a great chamber above, reached by another of Gwydir's many staircases studded with Maenan fragments. A pretty Elizabethan oriel window looks down into the courtyard from over the porch.

The dining room with its restored Jacobean panelling lies to the rear of the linking block. This is among the finest rooms of its period in Wales, *c*1640, precursor of the great Gilt Room at Tredegar (see page 115). Dark and glowing in any light, the walls are of rectangular panels with geometric dado treatment, below a frieze of embossed and silvered leather. At one end is a fireplace, at the other a door-case, both grandly baroque and reminiscent of a similar set in Wolfeton, in Dorset. Each is flanked by twinned spiral columns in the style of Bernini, said to indicate support for the Royalist cause.

The fireplace columns form a cornucopia from which tumble putti and birds. Heraldry and zoology drip from every corner. The door has a panel depicting a gryphon whose components, an eagle (front end) and lion (rear end), mischievously quote the Wynn quarterings.

Gwydir is gradually being refurnished with Elizabethan and Jacobean pieces. Medieval rooms with velvet hangings are already peopled with the ghosts of families long dead. Long tables and benches await wedding guests, their cries echoed by ubiquitous peacocks. Across the Conwy rolls a valley mist, above water meadows that present Gwydir with the menace of an occasional flood.

Harlech castle

★★☆ Fortress stronghold on rocky outcrop, taken by Owain Glyndwr

At Harlech, 5 miles S of Porthmadog; Cadw, open all year

Harlech is the definitive Welsh castle. It stands 200 feet high on an outcrop of the Rhinogs above Tremadog Bay, long painted and photographed with the bay and Snowdon in the distance. It suggests, wrote Jan Morris, 'such a gay glitter of flags and pageantry that the angriest Welsh separatist can hardly resist its charm.' Here we expect to find bards in full cry and damsels in distress. The difficulty with this view today is that politicians have allowed the Morfa dunes at the foot of the castle to be coated in a sprawl of bungalows, sheds and caravans. The humiliation of fortress Wales knows no bounds.

'The main castle ... appears to **rise straight from the rock** ...'

Left The main gate-passage was the principal entrance to Harlech's inner ward and as such was heavily defended. Any would-be attacker who tried to penetrate the gate-passage would have encountered a series of difficult obstacles. A wooden door secured by a heavy drawbar would have filled the first arch, and inside this would have been two portcullises, overlooked by arrowloops leading to the guardrooms. Then came another heavy door, opening onto the main length of the passage, with doorways off it to the guardrooms on either side. A final portcullis, and possibly another door, formed the final obstacle to the inner courtyard.

Harlech was built by the ubiquitous Master James of St George at the same time as Caernarfon and Conwy in the epic year of 1283. To the Welsh its claim to fame is in falling to Glyndwr in 1404 and becoming his military headquarters for the five years of his uprising. It was also held for the Lancastrians in the Wars of the Roses, enduring the longest siege (eight years) of those wars, the occasion of the song, *Men of Harlech*. It was also the last Royalist castle to surrender in the Civil War.

Harlech has a raw power less evident in other St George castles because it was crammed tight onto a crag. While technically a concentric plan on the Beaumaris pattern, the outer ward is merely a low wall hugging the cliff edge. The main castle thus appears to rise straight from the rock, with an impression of soaring impregnability rare even in Welsh castles. It is also in good condition.

Like Edward I's other castles, Harlech had to double as a house and garrison. The tight square of walls and corner towers embraced a fortified gatehouse that was both a keep and private chambers. The inner ward beyond contained the Great Hall, services and barracks. Guardianship of Harlech was conferred on St George as reward for his royal service. He was constable from 1290–93, a rare instance of an architect living in a building which he created for others. The inner parts of the castle apart from the gatehouse are mere footings.

Llanrwst almshouses

⭐ Jacobean almshouse, preserved as a museum

At Llanrwst, 10 miles S of Conwy; museum, open all year

A lane runs from Ancaster Square in the centre of Llanrwst to the church, lined on the right-hand side by a whitewashed Jacobean building with an enclosed courtyard behind. The almshouses were founded, with a free school, in 1610 by Sir Richard Wynn of Gwydir.

The charity was to maintain 12 men of the town (and women after 1843). It survived into the 19th century when, like many such foundations, it was ruined by corruption and mismanagement. Refounded in 1851, the charity lasted until the death in 1976 of the final inhabitant, Mary Delyn, widow of one of Llanrwst's many harpists. Of gypsy descent she spoke Romany as well as Welsh and would play the harp in the town square. The council declared the building unfit for habitation and was only just prevented from pulling it down.

Restoration as a museum began in 1996 and was completed in 2002. At first every room had been crammed with furniture, but museumitis took over and rendered the place immaculate. One room has been restored to its 17th-century appearance and another to the 19th century. Since the almshouses were the eventual home of so many Llanrwst harpists, it is a pity that such music cannot be heard in them today.

Lloyd George's boyhood home

⭐ Childhood home of the 'Welsh Wizard'

At Llanystumdwy, 4 miles W of Porthmadog; museum, open part year

The museum dedicated to the famous son of Llanystumdwy sits in the centre of the village opposite a smart chapel, Moriah, designed by Clough Williams-Ellis in 1936. It is filled with the customary paraphernalia of 20th-century history and statesmanship. More atmospheric is the neighbouring house where Lloyd George was raised.

After the death of his father, the young David Lloyd George and his siblings came to live at the simple two-up, two-down cottage named Highgate. It was owned by his mother's brother, Richard George, a cobbler, whose workshop is preserved downstairs. George was more than a cobbler. He was chapel elder, reader and intellectual, and his conversation while working on his boots was music to the young David's ears. A portrait of him in old age was commissioned by Lloyd George as a tribute. Such men are the unsung artisans of greatness.

Apart from the workshop, downstairs consisted of a kitchen/living room and formal parlour which became the children's study and contained the books left to them by their father. These books, revered by Lloyd George, are sadly now in the museum. The kitchen is as it was, with fire and range, cutlery and the usual contents of historic homes re-arranged for 'education'.

The family moved to Criccieth in 1880 and the house was sublet until 1969 when it was recovered and converted into the museum. A delightful cottage garden has been created to the rear, with a path to the garden privy or 'throne room'. On his death in 1945 Lloyd George chose to be buried not in Westminster Abbey but under the rock on which he used to sit and dream by the local stream, the Dwyfor. Here he could see the village bridge and his old school. He refused to allow even an inscription on the tomb.

Pennal: Cefn Caer

⭐ Medieval farmhouse, claimed as Glyndwr's home

At Pennal, 2½ miles W of Machynlleth; private house, open by arrangement

Whether or not Owain Glyndwr 'lived here' is, like most stories attaching to the man, moot. He would have passed this way from Harlech to the parliament believed to have been held at Machynlleth in 1404. More significant, a letter written two years later by his clerical aide, Gruffudd Young, requesting help from the king of France was dated from Pennal on 31st March, 1406, and is preserved in the French national archive. It offered to bring the Welsh church under the authority of the Avignon pope in return for papal recognition of a Welsh church distinct from that of England. The bid proved abortive, but gave plausibility to Pennal as a royal bed and breakfast.

Further evidence is adduced in the white farmhouse still standing on a hillock to the south of the village. The site is within the walls of a Roman camp and many Roman objects have surfaced over the years. The acquisition of the farm by the Rowlands family in the 1960s has led to its restoration, including the discovery of a 14th-century fireplace. It is here that the errant Glyndwr is supposed to have warmed his bones.

The enterprising owner, Elfyn Rowlands, has gone to great lengths to restore and uncover the history of the house. He is proud to show visitors round and holds medieval banquets in the hall, with guests in period costume. Pennal's equally enterprising vicar has less plausibly accorded the local church the status of 'chapel royal of the princes of Gwynedd'.

Cefn Caer is certainly an old Welsh hall house. The hall appears to have been divided in the Tudor period and given a new chimney, dated by the beams to *c*1525. What is remarkable is the survival behind it of the fireplace and chimney of the original house, with a double-arched opening dated *c*1490 and an old bread oven. The walls have Roman tiles presumably gathered from the fields outside. A dais screen is decorated with an owl, a kestrel and human figures.

The house is filled with furniture and objects of the period, including dressers, pewter and a reproduction table with benches. Outside are splendid views over the Dyfi valley, familiar to me from regular visits to this village since childhood.

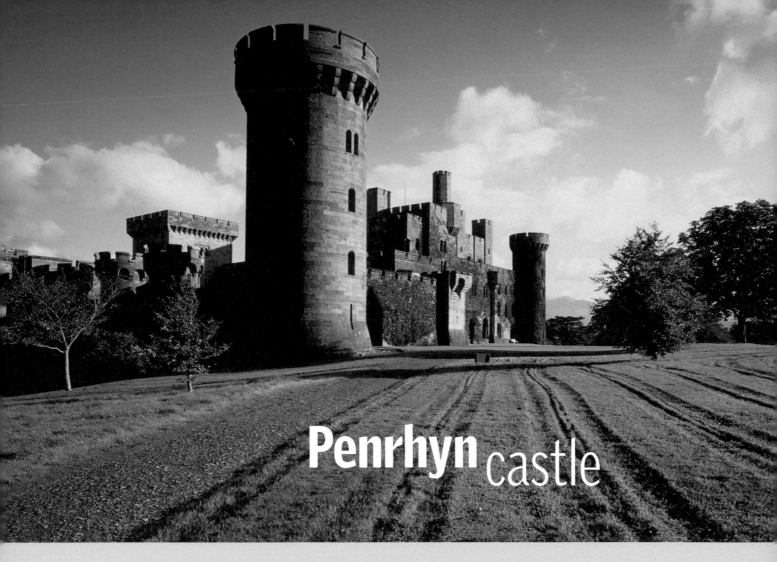

Penrhyn castle

★★★☆ Grand Victorian mansion and supreme example of neo-Norman style

At Llandygai, 1 mile E of Bangor; National Trust, open part year

Penrhyn is one of the greatest Victorian houses, and surely the least known. As a work of architectural romanticism it stands comparison with Windsor, Arundel and Eastnor. As a work of Norman revival it is in a class of its own. The creator, Lord Penrhyn, spent half a million pounds on its construction, over a hundred million today, yet he appears not to have batted an eyelid. His was the greatest slate mine in the world, at neighbouring Bethesda, with sugar estates in the West Indies to match. Two Penrhyn daughters were nicknamed Sugar and Slate in honour of the family's wealth.

The original estate belonged to the Griffiths of Anglesey, with a medieval manor house set on a promontory overlooking the Menai Straits opposite Beaumaris. This was sold in 1622 and passed to an Englishman, John Williams, who was a descendant of an earlier owner named Gwylim, from whom it passed by marriage to a family of wealthy merchants, the Pennants of Flintshire.

The 18th-century Richard Pennant, later 1st Baron Penrhyn (1739–1808), was Wales's answer to Coke of Norfolk, an improver, entrepreneur and politician. His slate quarry benefited from his salesmanship of 'slates' as a standard school writing material. He also championed the sugar industry and defended the slave trade as a Liverpool MP. Pennant was so rich that when slate went into recession he redirected his workforce from quarrying to construction to await an upturn, building an early tramway from Bethesda to Port Penrhyn. With the boom in domestic tourism during the French wars, he also built hotels for visitors to Snowdonia at Capel Curig and Bethesda.

'The interior might be an epic movie set ...'

Above The billiard table in the library at Penrhyn is believed to be unique. It is constructed of enamelled slate and was made by George Eugene Magnus, the owner of a North Wales slate quarry, as a gift for Colonel Douglas-Pennant to demonstrate the enamelling technique he had developed.

Pennant employed the ubiquitous Wyatt family as managers and architects. Samuel Wyatt built estate villas and extended the old castle on the cliff, while his brother, Benjamin, designed villages, avenues and bathing pools. By the time Pennant died in 1808 he had transformed north Caernarfonshire from a wild hill farming community to a prosperous landscape of new roads, villages and resorts. His memorial is in Llandegai church, a sarcophagus attended by a quarryman and a farm girl.

Pennant was childless and bequeathed his estate to a distant cousin, George Dawkins (1764–1840), on condition that he add Pennant to his name. Dawkins was MP for Newark and though he had to wait until 1816 and the death of Pennant's wife to assume his inheritance, he did so in style. Wyatt's old gothick house he considered out of date, not to mention too small. Gwrych Castle had already been completed for another Lancashire plutocrat, Bamford-Hesketh, along the coast at Abergele. This had to be outdone.

Why Dawkins-Pennant chose Thomas Hopper as architect and romantic neo-Norman as the style remains obscure. Hopper had worked for the Prince Regent but had designed little of substance. Conscious of Welsh history, he avoided the gothic of Edward I, choosing instead the style of Wales's earlier invaders, the Normans. Building began about 1820 and continued to 1835.

Penrhyn is gigantically Norman, a fairy-tale composition of keep, towers, turrets, wings and service ranges. The old medieval manor was not demolished but rather engulfed. The service ranges constitute a castle in themselves. Most remarkable, Dawkins-Pennant insisted that the building materials and craftsmen (apart from stained glass) be local.

The design was not castellated pastiche but properly defensive, defying Pugin's complaint that most Regency castles were so domestic that an assailant could 'kick his way in through the conservatory'. The castle came complete with arrow slits and murder holes. There were also hot air ducts, oil and later gas lights, lavatories and an early system of hot and cold running water to the bathrooms.

The creator of this splendour lived barely four years after its completion and was buried in Oxfordshire. The house passed through a daughter to another English family, the Douglases (perforce becoming Douglas-Pennants). They continued to expand the estate, acquired a major art collection and lived in the castle, where they entertained Queen Victoria, the Prince of Wales and Gladstone. Penrhyn passed to the National Trust in 1951.

The interior might be an epic movie set, except that Hopper never seems to lose stylistic control. The quality of carving and craftsmanship renders every corner a museum piece. Norman is everywhere, from window openings and vaults to fireplaces and chair backs. An entrance gallery leads into the Grand Hall. Stone vaulted and aisled, it is like the chancel of a 12th-century cathedral, rich in shafted columns and dogtooth carving. One visitor described it as 'about as homely as a great railway terminus … or an exhibition of locomotives or dinosaurs'. Lofty windows are filled with Willement's finest neo-medieval glass.

From here the plan of the house is clear. A passageway to the left leads to the family bedrooms in the great keep while to the right stretch the state rooms, expanded from those of the former manor. The latter are formed of the library, drawing room and ebony room. Here Hopper struggled to domesticate his Norman tendencies. Arches are flattened, windows expanded and not an inch is free of swirls, dogtooth, nail-head and geometrical carving. The ceiling bosses declare Dawkins-Pennant's (distant) ancestral title to the place. Each door-case, fireplace, table and settee is an individual creation, carved with mummers, animals and heraldic beasts. Axminster carpets cover the floors and the curtains and furnishings are of silk.

Between the drawing room (on the site of the manorial hall) and the ebony room is an entrance to a medieval spiral staircase and to a lost tower. The ebony room, used as the ladies' drawing room, takes its name from the veneered and fake ebony of the arches and the furniture, their rich brown/black enhanced by velvet upholstery.

'As a work of Norman revival it is **in a class of its own.'**

The main staircase is Hopper's virtuoso piece, a vertical shaft of interlaced Norman arches, real and blind, rising to an oriental lantern. The walls display motifs taken from pattern books of ancient architecture and medieval sports and pastimes. Each capital appears different, even in its stone.

Upstairs a ghostly passage leads back to the keep, modelled on Hedingham Castle in Essex. Here are the family rooms, arranged as a suite on each floor. In one is the slate bed in which Queen Victoria famously refused to sleep on her first visit. Wallpapers are by William Morris. The state bedroom has heavy coffered ceilings yet delicate furnishings, including Chinese wallpaper. The furniture and pictures are all in place, remarkably intact after the vicissitudes of the 20th century. The wallpaper in the Lower India Room is glorious Regency chinoiserie.

Two spectaculars remain. In the chapel Hopper risks exaggeration. The dogtooth vaulting comes down to shoulder height to join piers coated in zigzag. Not an inch is left flat and the room is suffused with light from stained glass by David Evans of Shrewsbury. The dining room is near indigestible in its richness. The ceiling might be that of a medieval Florentine palazzo enhanced, says the guide, 'by the study of West Indian botanical forms'. The walls carry stencilled Norman motifs while the dado is carved of wood with intersecting arcading.

Walls throughout are hung with paintings from the Penrhyn collection, by Teniers, van der Neer, Gainsborough, Ramsay and a large group portrait of the Dawkins family, with the builder of the castle as a boy. In the breakfast room next door are works by Holbein, Rembrandt, Palma Vecchio, Canaletto and van der Velde. Penrhyn is the Welsh national gallery of the north, yet how many know it?

The familiar offices of a great house are at Penrhyn doubled in scale. To the normal services are added an ice tower, a dung tower and, for good measure, a railway museum. These now form an attraction separate from the house.

Above The saloon at Plas Newydd is on the ground floor of the round tower, which was added in 1751; a semi-circular bay window looks out over the Menai Strait. The decoration dates from the 1930s, when the 6th Marquess of Anglesey and his wife had the room rearranged to accommodate four large landscapes, painted *c*1789 by Balthasar Paul Ommeganck. The 6th Marquess was Queen Mary's Lord Chamberlain for 22 years, and photographs of Queen Mary and George V are still displayed on the writing table.

Plas Newydd

★ ★ ★ ☆ Gothick house in beautiful location, with paintings by Rex Whistler

Near Llanfairpwll, 4 miles SW of Bangor; National Trust, open part year

Everything in the Marquess of Anglesey's house on the Menai Straits is subordinate to its setting. Where others have an approach avenue, Plas Newydd has an exotic descent through beeches, limes and sub-tropical vegetation. Where others have terraces overlooking lakes, Plas Newydd has the strait rushing back and forth. Where others might have a hill in the distance, Plas Newydd has the massed majesty of Snowdon.

The medieval house belonged to the Griffiths of Penrhyn in the 1470s, descending through the Bayly family to the present marquess via the titles of Lord Paget and the Earl of Uxbridge. It was Sir Henry Bayly who, in the 1780s and 1790s, began the rebuilding of the house in a style variously neo-gothic (usually termed gothick) and neo-classical, principally to the designs of James Wyatt. There is also a Repton Red Book for the layout of the grounds, dated 1799. The exterior was 'un-gothicked' in the 1930s when the interior was reordered for a grand mural by Rex Whistler.

Though owned by the National Trust, Plas Newydd is still occupied and cared for by the 7th Marquess of Anglesey, who succeeded to the title in 1947. He is the descendant of the 1st Marquess who was head of Wellington's cavalry, lost his leg at Waterloo and is commemorated in a Nelsonian column on the hill behind the house.

On first view, the exterior is an anticlimax. The style is over-altered and in gunmetal grey render, which looks good neither in sun nor in rain. Its virtue is that, unlike Penrhyn, it does not try to be what it is not.

The approach is past a field in the middle of which is a large cromlech. There are too many trees shrouding the first glimpses of the house and a visit is best begun on the terrace where we can see

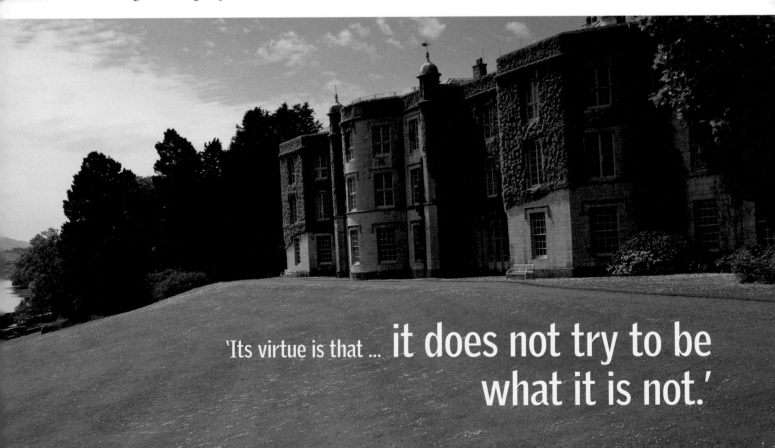

'Its virtue is that ... it does not try to be what it is not.'

Above In 1936 the 6th Marquess commissioned Rex Whistler to paint murals for a new dining room he was having created on the ground floor of the north wing. Whistler painted the main mural on one piece of canvas, 58 feet long. He worked on the painting in a theatre workshop in London before bringing it out to Plas Newydd in June 1937.

what Wyatt was seeking to exploit. The wooded land across the strait opposite, that of the Vaynol estate, has been bought by the National Trust to protect the view.

The entrance is into Wyatt's so-called Gothick Hall, spare and chapel-like but with a lierne and fan plaster vault and delicate gallery at the far end. The chamber is naked but was once crammed with pennants, banners, armour, chinoiserie and a stuffed bear. It needs them.

Next is the Music Room, Wyatt's Plas Newydd masterpiece, though the execution was by Joseph Potter of Lichfield. The delicate fan vault perfectly matches the proportions of the windows. A conversation piece by Rex Whistler shows the family in 1938 (including the present marquess as a painter), all looking rather bored. A Lawrence of the 1st Marquess in full Hussar rig hangs on the wall.

The staircase hall is austerely Doric, adorned with military portraits and landscapes and leading to the upper floor. This is conventionally domestic, though Lord Anglesey's bedroom contains a state bed, covered in exquisite Chinese silk with flower patterns, repeated in the pelmet over the windows. This and adjacent rooms are full of sea pictures, appropriate to the view from the windows.

The ground floor rooms on the 'view' side have been much reorganized and are of interest chiefly for the homely arrangement of pictures and furniture. Light floods them all. Large landscape pictures suit the marriage of architecture and outlook that is a feature of the house.

The enfilade culminates in two rooms dedicated to Whistler, a friend of the family who stayed often at Plas Newydd, where he painted his last and one of his greatest capriccios (rivalling Port Lympne in Kent). It is of canvas glued to the plaster and fills the wall of what was the dining room. It depicts a series of famous buildings – Windsor Castle, St Martin-in-the-Field, Trajan's Column – as if they were outside the window of Plas Newydd. Overhead are billowing clouds and in the foreground symbolic objects, such as Poseidon's trident, the family dog and Whistler himself as a gardener.

Plas yn Rhiw

Near Rhiw, 22 miles SW of Porthmadog; National Trust, open part year

Former owners of Plas yn Rhiw claimed continuous descent from the 9th-century kings of Powys to 1874. The house was then abandoned until acquired by the three Keating sisters of Nottingham in 1938. They restored it, re-created the Victorian garden and gave everything to the National Trust in 1946, one sister living here until 1981.

The most prominent feature of the house is its location, near the tip of the Llyn peninsula overlooking Hell's Mouth Bay. Like all views on the Llyn, on a fine day it is beyond compare, sweeping the full extent of Cardigan Bay to Strumble Head. Open to the Gulf Stream and shielded from the north and east it is an ideal place for the shrubs and flowers that fill the garden to bursting.

The Keatings engaged Clough Williams-Ellis to help them acquire the house and restore it. They also set up the Council for the Protection of Rural Wales, much needed in these parts. Williams-Ellis's minor work on the interior offers the chief interest in what is a modest home.

The entrance is into a small hall dating back to the house's 17th-century origins. Williams-Ellis adorned it with oak columns, plaster capitals and a gothic door-case, known as 'Cloughing it up'. The parlour, staircase and upstairs rooms are filled with Keating *objets trouvés*. These include family portraits, pewter, furniture, and paintings and watercolours of Wales. There is an early Teasmaid in the bedroom.

From the upstairs sitting room is a view out over box, yew and rhododendron to the deep blue of Hell's Mouth Bay. Here as often as not can be seen the reason for its name, the foaming anger of a storm that brought many ships to ruin.

'... shrubs and flowers ... **fill the garden to bursting.**'

Portmeirion village

★★★ Adventurous work of 20th-century picturesque architecture

At Portmeirion, 2 miles SE of Porthmadog; private houses, open all year

The view north across Cardigan Bay from Harlech embraces a harmony of water, wood and mountain with, on the distant shore, what appears a Mediterranean mirage of village campanile. This is Portmeirion, creation of the 20th-century architect, Clough Williams-Ellis and never free of controversy. Portmeirion has been variously dismissed as un-Welsh, continental, tropical, pastiche, a stylistic junk-yard and, worst of all, popular. The settlement was begun in 1926 and mostly completed by 1976. It thus straddled the modernist era, at which it thumbed its nose. Most visitors regard it as no more than enjoyably festive. To Williams-Ellis it was more significant, and justly so.

The site was bought in 1925 for £5,000. It consisted of a forest of semi-ornamental trees behind a Victorian villa on the shore, with a steep rocky ravine next to it. Here Williams-Ellis planned his township. He was not intending a joke, nor was he trying to import an Italian language to jolly up a Welsh resort. He understood that the jumbled settlements of the Mediterranean derived their communal quality by deferring buildings to context and contour. Modern architecture might be averse to colonnades, arches, terraces, gazebos, towers and intimate public spaces, but that did not make these things foreign.

Each Portmeirion house, many saved from demolition elsewhere in Wales, has its personal rock or defile, linked to others by steps and terraces. Movement round the village is on foot, cars being unusable here. There is elegance to Portmeirion and a constant visual surprise, well captured by its use as the set for the television series *The Prisoner* (whose cult is honoured in a small museum).

PORTMEIRION

Above The American architect Frank Lloyd Wright (on the right) was an admirer of Clough Williams-Ellis (on the left); the two had met in the 1930s on a train from Berlin to Moscow and are pictured here during Lloyd Wright's visit to Portmeirion in 1956.
Right The Toll House in Portmeirion's Battery Square was built in 1929; the painted statue on the balcony is of St Peter.

Williams-Ellis intended Portmeirion as a holiday village. He restored the waterfront villa as a hotel and continued with cottages to let, each with some foible reflected in its name: Battery, Toll House, Prior's Lodging, Government House, Watch House and Lady's Lodge. Each was embellished with an architectural distinction, such as a Dutch gable, pantiles, a Baroque doorcase, a Regency window.

Of the early buildings the one obviously Italianate structure was the bell tower, intended by Williams-Ellis to 'open my performance with a dramatic gesture'. While it clearly echoes Portofino in Italy it also echoes an English church. The buildings are almost all coloured in a bright, cheerful stucco, an East Anglian touch that is undeniably unusual among the grey slate villages of Snowdonia. This again was considered 'un-Welsh'.

After the Second World War Williams-Ellis became more ambitious, deciding to extend Portmeirion into 'a home for fallen buildings'.

The Town Hall (see page 160) came from Emral in Flintshire. The Gloriette, Gothic Pavilion, Bristol Colonnade and Pantheon were all salvages. Williams-Ellis's genius was in marrying these elements into a theatrical whole by relating them to a series of public spaces, as in any informal village. I have seen Portmeirion in all weathers and elements and it never fails to delight the eye.

Portmeirion's tragedy was to be so ridiculed by professional architects as to render repetition anathema. Its use of sculpture and murals, mosaics, plaques, and even a statue of Shakespeare on a balcony, seemed to reduce architecture to whimsy. The Prince of Wales's mild homage to Portmeirion at his Poundbury estate outside Dorchester suffered similar obloquy. 'Another Portmeirion' became a term of abuse.

While the village is an amused variation on architectural themes, it reflects a sophisticated aesthetic eye and the hand of a craftsman. Williams-Ellis professed to 'a natural instinct for responding to a site or a building's requirements appropriately … an unerring judgment for proportion and a weakness for splendour and display.' The proof is in the eating. Portmeirion must be the only 20th-century town in Europe which 200,000 people a year pay just to visit.

The Town Hall ✫

The most remarkable of the 'salvage' buildings stands on the far side of the village where the road runs down to the hotel. It was Williams-Ellis's most developed creation, round the rescued Great Hall of 17th-century Emral Hall in Flintshire.

Its treasure is the most glorious Jacobean ceiling surviving in Wales, barrel-vaulted and depicting the labours of Hercules in plaster. This was on the brink of destruction in 1937 when Williams-Ellis rescued it for £13. He had to dismantle and remove not just the ceiling but much of the house with it, including mullioned windows reused for the opera house cum community centre.

While the building's appeal is in these imports, it remains a Williams-Ellis building. The ground floor is of stone, the upper floors a pale terracotta wash. Windows and doors are reminiscent of Frank Lloyd Wright (who admired Portmeirion), yet the roof lantern with a crown on top of a pig boiler is pure Williams-Ellis. Inside is his bust by Jonah Jones, a Durham sculptor who settled in Wales and went on to become principal of Dublin School of Art. He contributed many of the plaques and statues at Portmeirion. The Town Hall, like all of Portmeirion, embodies qualities that should move all architecture: a respect for creations of the past and an ability to set those creations in a new context.

Below Williams-Ellis read about the planned demolition of Emral Hall in *Country Life* and resolved to save its Jacobean ceiling. He ended up rescuing many of its other architectural features that also found their way into his village.

PORTMEIRION

Ty Hyll

⋆⋆ Simple medieval home, known as the 'Ugly House'

At Capel Curig, 4 miles W of Betws-y-Coed; private house, open all year

This extraordinary structure is an example of Darwin's survival of the fittest. Ancient law stated that anyone who could build a house in a night and have smoke coming from its chimney by morning would enjoy squatters' rights. Hence the nickname 'ty'r nos' or house of the night. The builder could also claim a smallholding to the extent that he could throw an axe from each corner of the building.

There were once many such buildings in Wales but this is the only one to survive in recognizable form, built in 1475 by two outlaw brothers. It is inconceivable that it can have been built in a night, but it may have been constructed of turf and then rebuilt, and there was often goodwill from manorial authorities eager for immigrants.

The wall stones are undressed slabs from the mountain outside, positioned so the rain would fall outwards. For mortar there would have been moss, traces of which have been found in the walls. The roof would initially have been of logs covered in heather thatch. The lack of any 'finish' is what gives the house its name, curiosity and charm. Only the later slate roof indicates modernity.

The story of the house is lost. It was abandoned when workers on Telford's Holyhead road came upon it in 1815 and stayed in it for the duration of their work. There was no census reference but a Victorian guide of 1853 mentions it as 'one of the most picturesque cottages imaginable ... giving additional beauty to this romantic dell'.

The house was later visited by tourists to Snowdonia, occupied first by a shepherd and then by a Great War veteran named Riley who invented himself as 'the little crooked man in the little crooked house' of the children's rhyme. He and his wife died in the 1960s. The house fell on hard times until taken over by the Snowdonia Society in 1988 as part office and shop, part Welsh cottage museum. The garden is still mercifully wild.

Ty Mawr

★★★ Tudor farmhouse and birthplace of pioneering translator of the Bible

3 miles S of Betws-y-Coed; National Trust, open part year

'The spot is **idyllic.**'

Ty Mawr was the birthplace of William Morgan, translator of the Bible into Welsh. It is an old farmhouse beautifully situated in an isolated corner of the Wybrnant valley, tributary of the Conwy four miles south of Betws-y-coed.

Morgan's life typified the Tudor Welsh ascendancy. He was born the second son of a farmer in 1545 and brought up conversant with the verse and song of Wales. Showing early promise he came under the patronage of the Wynns of Gwydir and made his way to St John's College, Cambridge, returning as vicar of Llanbadarn Fawr and Welshpool, a classic case of upwards social mobility. It is a measure of the decline of Anglicanism in Tudor Wales that, in 1587, only three of the 134 parishes in St Asaph diocese had resident incumbents. One reason was Henry VIII's decree that only English be used in church, a language few worshippers would have understood.

Morgan's work on the Bible was preceded by that of William Salesbury and others who translated the prayer book and New Testament into antique Welsh. Morgan preferred a more contemporary language, only marred, says the guide, 'by occasional traces of North Wales dialect'. He completed his translation in 1587 and went to London to supervise the printing (and proof-reading). Some 1,000 copies of his Bibles were printed.

The Morgan Bible was astonishingly popular. Despite editing and revision it has survived unaltered, while the English Bible was being 'authorized and revised'. Not until 1988 was a new text published, and Morgan's creation still lies massive and majestic on lecterns, tables and dressers across Wales. He rose to become Bishop of St Asaph and died in 1604.

Ty Mawr is a conventional Tudor farmhouse, but more substantial than that in which Morgan was born, which would have been of just one storey with a hall open to the roof. In the rebuilding of the late-Elizabethan period a fireplace and upper chambers were inserted. Later alterations were removed when the house passed to the National Trust and was restored to its early 17th-century state.

The house has a screens passage, hall and upper bedroom. The furniture is contemporary with, but not original to, the house. Part of the upstairs is devoted to a museum of Welsh Bibles. The flowers round the outside are of the 16th century and an old byre has been left on the other bank of the stream. The spot is idyllic.

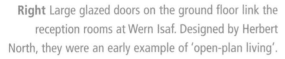

Wern Isaf

Right Large glazed doors on the ground floor link the reception rooms at Wern Isaf. Designed by Herbert North, they were an early example of 'open-plan living'.

✮✮ Arts-and-Crafts house of the early 20th century

Near Llanfairfechan, 5 miles SW of Conwy; private house, open part year

This rare example of a 'butterfly' house sits on a hillside outside Bangor, looking across the Menai Strait to Anglesey. It is inhabited by the granddaughter of its architect, Herbert North, an English immigrant to Wales who worked for Lutyens and was a pupil of the Arts-and-Crafts master, Henry Wilson. He co-authored pioneering works on the churches and cottages of Snowdonia.

The house is charmingly set in woods above a meadow. It was built in 1900 and has been preserved to convey the self-conscious ideology of its period. The concept of the butterfly was to emphasize the line from the entrance through a staircase lobby and out on the far side into nature. The rooms were set at an angle to this axis, like the wings of an insect.

Such a house was meant, said the architectural theorist, William Lethaby, to derive a *genius loci* from this arrangement. North's house even has a crystal ball hanging in the hall to carry its spirit from the front door through the French windows at the back to a pool on the far terrace. He said it needed 'the element of beauty and poetry which gives it individuality … the relations of window to wall, of chimneys to roof, of mass to contour – a beauty for which many of the old cottages are so conspicuous.'

The entrance hall is in white wood, dominated by stairs which rise to a landing giving access to all bedrooms. There is thus no need of a space-wasting corridor. The downstairs is composed of a curved sequence of living rooms looking out into the garden. They can be combined as one volume or divided by partitions into four. The window seats are repeated in the seats of the terrace outside. Delightful wooden shutters carry patterned cut-outs, declining in number as they approach the kitchen.

Everything original has been retained, cupboards, furniture, tables and fireplace surrounds, some decorated with lozenge patterns, others with ceramic or mother-of-pearl. North's wife, Ida, was a keen needlewoman and her work is displayed everywhere, along with alcoves containing pots and other objects of the period. North designed Wern Isaf when he was just 28 and died in 1941; it retains the atmosphere of a young man's fancy.

Powys

Powis Castle

Powys

Abbey-cwm-hir

★★ Restored late 19th-century house with extensive collection of Victoriana

At Abbey-cwm-hir, 10 miles N of Llandrindod Wells; private house, open by arrangement

The only way to approach the new Abbey-cwm-hir is on its own terms. A Victorian mansion of Alpine/Transylvanian demeanour sits among trees in one of the most entrancing valleys of mid Wales. Here the Cistercians built what was intended to be their largest and most isolated abbey, larger even than Tintern. Today all that remains are cursory ruins along the valley floor.

Over this presides the house bought by Paul and Victoria Humpherson in 1997, restored as a home and museum of Victoriana, though museum hardly does justice to the growing hysteria I felt as I was guided round its 52 rooms. The place is crammed with impedimenta until, in the basement and conservatory, it explodes into rampant kitsch. The place is astonishing. Abbey-cwm-hir is a Victorian version of the Dennis Severs house in London's Spitalfields.

The old farmhouse was built for a family named Philips in 1869 by the architects, Poundley and Walker. The style reflects the transition from early Victorian formality to the freer eclecticism of Burges and then Art Nouveau. The Humphersons have restored the plasterwork, fireplaces, floor tiles and staircase, with decorative additions to doors, woodwork and wallpaper by Victoria Humpherson. Modern paintings of the house in all weathers start from the walls. Everywhere is Paul Humpherson's Staffordshire pottery, he being from Stoke-on-Trent.

After the formal rooms, the magpies let rip. The library is of early editions of children's adventure books, a wonderful collection. The billiard room is stencilled with the names of Arthur's knights – Abbey-cwm-hir being a candidate for Camelot – and full of stuffed animals. One kitchen laden with paraphernalia leads to another likewise. Bedrooms are perfectly laid out as if awaiting guests, with pyjamas folded and ready.

Rooms are variously 'themed' to ocean liners, armies, planes, motorbikes. Cupboards are full of clothes. Cabinets and bars are full of drink. There is a traffic sign here, a wall of whisky bottles there and a mass of early advertising placards. Everything is spotless, not least the walled garden which stretches up the hillside to the rear.

Abercamlais

Above It was a Thomas Williams who created the house now seen at Abercamlais. In 1710 he commissioned a new façade and re-ordered and redecorated the interiors in a suitably Georgian style. The drawing room (above right) has a baroque-style plasterwork ceiling and magnificent fireplace; both are believed to have come from elsewhere, the fireplace reputedly from William Beckford's home at Fonthill.

★ ★ Georgian gentry house with unusual outbuilding over a stream

5 miles W of Brecon; private house, open by arrangement

The house sits on the banks of the River Usk at its loveliest, upstream of Brecon. Next door is the rival Williams family mansion of Penpont. The latter is a severely classical Regency composition, possibly by Smirke, but inaccessible. Abercamlais is early Georgian and carries its years well. The house has been occupied by Williamses since Tudor times, all but one of whom from 1570 to 1935 were in holy orders. The exception became a high sheriff. The house is still occupied by a Williams, Susan Ballance.

What had been a farmhouse was given a three-storey Georgian front when the family came into money in 1710. Apart from the addition of dormers in the roof, the house is now much as it was built. Identical windows spread across seven bays, unrelieved by string courses or pilasters and undeniably severe.

The Victorian porch was designed by a family friend, the youthful George Gilbert Scott. The effect is of subdued tranquillity.

The interior is contemporary with the house, a series of Georgian rooms round a central hall with the staircase tucked behind. The drawing room fireplace is reputed to have come from the sale of Fonthill Abbey. The baroque plasterwork in the ceiling here and in the hall is probably also imported.

An intriguing Georgian pigeon house stands in the grounds directly over a stream. The upper part is a dovecote but the latrine below gives directly into the water. It is not clear how this related to the house plumbing. The environs of Abercamlais, its bridge, kitchen garden, woods and drive suggest centuries of careful husbandry. Until the railway closed in 1962, the house even had its own request stop.

Craig-y-nos

★★ Baronial-style mansion and refuge of Victorian operatic diva

At Pen-y-cae, 12 miles NE of Neath; now a hotel

The Italian, Adelina Patti (1843–1919), was the most famous opera singer of her age. She performed before emperors, tsars, monarchs and tycoons and was paid 5,000 gold dollars for one performance of *La Traviata* in Boston. In St Petersburg she was carried by six generals on a seat of flowers to her hotel after a show. The daughter of a Sicilian and a Roman, she first married Napoleon's equerry, then a French tenor, Ernest Nicolini, then at the age of 56 a 30-year-old Swedish 'nobleman and masseur'. So how did she come to live in a dark and wet corner of the Brecon Beacons, in a house with the Wagnerian name of the 'rock of the night'?

The answer appears to lie with another wealthy admirer, Lord Swansea. He took Patti on a tour of the Beacons and showed her an old manor clinging to the edge of a ravine. He suggested it as a refuge from her tours. In addition Patti, then aged 35, needed relief from polluted city air that was upsetting her lungs. Here she could walk for hours and breathe the zephyrs of the Beacons. She fell for the place, arriving in 1878 with her lover and second husband-to-be, the French tenor.

The house had been built by T. H. Wyatt in the 1840s, but his work was drastically extended by Patti in a Scots-baronial style, with towers, turrets and gables, by Bucknall and Jennings of Swansea. Ten years later she added a small concert hall in the style of a London opera house, in gold, cream and peach. The walls of this Welsh Bayreuth are adorned with classical pilasters, the auditorium is raked and a backdrop shows Patti in her favourite role, on a chariot as Handel's Semiramis.

Above The theatre that opera singer Adelina Patti had built at Craig-y-nos opened on 12 July, 1891. It had a range of innovative features and was the first theatre to have electric stage lighting. The auditorium floor could be raised to the same level as the stage, thus turning the theatre into a ballroom; the original mechanism is still in working order.
Below The Music Room contains mementos of Patti's career, including portraits and photographs.

Patti gave free performances here to anyone who could make their way up the mountain. They flocked, including the Prince of Wales and impresarios eager to sign her for their theatres. She had her own waiting room at Penwyllt station. When she arrived local people would form a guard of honour for her carriage up to Craig-y-nos. She died here in 1919 but was buried in Père-Lachaise in Paris. The house fell on hard times and was for a long time a TB sanatorium and then geriatric hospital.

Craig-y-nos is now a wedding hotel, crudely publicized and with few echoes of its past. Bucknall and Jennings' work appears devoid of merit, being rich and vulgar, though this may be later alterations. The rooms still have pictures and mementos of Patti and the theatre survives, used occasionally by Patti fans for operatic revivals. The reception rooms offer spectacular views over the ravine of the River Tawe. The place is certainly within bounds of redemption.

Gregynog

Near Tregynon, 6 miles N of Newtown; private house, open by arrangement

Ramparts of trees line the drive to the big house, which lies hidden in a dripping Welsh jungle. It was reconstructed from a 17th century original by Charles Hanbury-Tracy, later 1st Baron Sudeley, in 1837 and completed by his son in the 1860s. The house was one of the first anywhere to be made of the new building material of concrete (un-reinforced), as were many cottages on the estate. It is a Victorian grandee's pastiche of how a Midlands black-and-white mansion might look, if double the normal size. The cottages are concrete *cottages ornés*.

The house had various owners until bought by Gwendoline and Margaret Davies, from the Montgomeryshire village of Llandinam and heiresses to one of Wales's greatest fortunes, that of the coal and railway town of Barry. They became champions of French art and Welsh culture, and lobbied on behalf of the Glamorganshire poor during the Depression.

The Davies sisters were among the first Britons to appreciate the Impressionists, notably Cezanne. Their collection, mostly amassed during the Great War, now graces the National Museum of Wales in Cardiff. The sisters intended Gregynog to be a Welsh centre of the Arts-and-Crafts movement, setting up a music room, art gallery and printing press. The last is still in being. The house was bequeathed to the University of Wales in 1960 as a residential centre, where the Davies tradition is maintained.

Gregynog is chiefly magnificent for its setting. A dip lies in front of the main terrace, once destined as a lake and now a parterre of yews. Beyond rises a stupendous wall of rhododendron and pine, which in the right light can seem like a tidal wave of green surf advancing on the house.

From here, Gregynog looks like a cardboard stage set, or at least a concrete one. Painted black and white strips are intended to make the concrete walls look like wood and plaster, close-studded and with decorative quatrefoils. The three storeys are all of the same proportion and the gables are too small. Haslam in *Pevsner* concludes that 'the result does not quite escape absurdity or even plain awfulness, yet it is masculine and in a way logical'.

One room of the former Jacobean house survives as the Blayney Room, named after the original owners, its panelling and fireplace dated 1636. The rest of the interior is Victorian and institutionalized, though some works from the Davies collection remain on display.

Hay-on-Wye castle

★ ★ Eccentric castle with surviving Norman keep and Jacobean mansion

At Hay-on-Wye, 13 miles SE of Builth Wells; private house, open all year

Hay and its castle are in every sense eccentric. The old town sits astride the English border and in 1977 was declared an autonomous 'kingdom' by its presiding genius, Richard Booth, admittedly on April Fool's Day. From the castle he ruled both his kingdom and, more important, the evolution of Hay into the world's first book town. He awarded dukedoms, earldoms and peerages and fought (and still fights) battles against bureaucracy. His booklets have such titles as 'Bring back Horses' and 'God Save Us from the Development Board for Wales'.

The old castle still dominates the town, with fine views up and down the spacious Wye valley beneath Hay Bluff. This was unusually turbulent Powys, with seven castles within two miles. The original structure of Hay replaced a motte and bailey on a knoll and was regularly burned or sacked in Anglo-Welsh conflicts. It succumbed to ruination in the Wars of the Roses but the keep survives, with Norman windows, a Norman door and later Tudor insertions.

The most prominent feature of the castle, and of Hay, is the Jacobean mansion built onto the side of the keep in the 1660s. Its tall brick chimneys and Dutch-gabled roof rise above the old mound. After frequent changes of ownership it was extensively restored by Caroe in 1910 but the interior was destroyed by a fire in 1939, including the Jacobean staircase and fittings.

Booth bought the castle as a ruin in the 1960s, restored it and then saw it again gutted by fire in 1978. Restoration is proceeding, but only the main rooms are accessible and they are full of books. Indeed wherever you look in Hay are books. The terraces of the castle during the annual Hay festival take on the form of a literary soukh, only adding to the scruffy charm of the place.

Llanfyllin: The Council house

⭐ Prisoner's murals surviving from the Napoleonic war

At Llanfyllin, 9 miles NW of Welshpool; private house, open by arrangement

The Georgian property is adjacent to and occupied by Llanfyllin's chemist. The house, built in the 1740s, was used to incarcerate captured French officers during the Napoleonic war in 1811–13, their arrival causing a stir among the ladies of the village. They were confined to a mile radius and could attend a local dance only by the discreet moving of an offending milepost.

The inmate of The Council House, Lieutenant Pierre Augeraud, duly fell in love with the rector's daughter of the church opposite. The alarmed rector secured his immediate release and he was sent back to France. But love conquered freedom and when hostilities were over he returned and eloped with the girl. They lived happily in France ever after. Their Augeraud descendants still return to see the house.

It was during his initial stay that Augeraud painted murals over the walls of his upstairs room. Using sheep-marker dye and formalin, he evoked a romantic landscape of mountains and lakes in various shades of blue. The work is of mediocre quality but charming and well preserved. It is Llanfyllin's most remarkable war memorial.

Right Lieutenant Pierre Augeraud was one of 148 soldiers held captive in Llanfyllin during the Napoleonic war. He passed his time as a prisoner by painting picturesque landscapes on the walls of his temporary home.

Llangoed hall

⭐ Arts-and-Crafts transformation of a Jacobean manor

Near Llyswen, 8 miles NE of Brecon; now a hotel

The old house of the Williams family is now a smart hotel much patronized during the Hay festival. Built in 1632 (or rebuilt on the site of a reputed Welsh parliament) it has been remodelled inside but retains the appearance of a Jacobean E-plan house outside. Over the door is a stone depicting the Williams's three cocks. The present owner is Sir Bernard Ashley, husband of the late Laura Ashley, who rescued the house from demolition in 1987.

The appeal of the hall derives from its rebuilding in 1913 by Clough Williams-Ellis. It was his first major work in the Lutyens/*Country Life* tradition of manorial restoration. Hence the steep hipped roofs and dormer windows, as if the architect had taken a 17th-century mansion and clapped an Arts-and-Crafts one on top of it. This act of architectural millinery required steel girders to support it. The façade is now covered in Virginia creeper.

The interior displays more of Williams-Ellis's Lutyens humour, with only the library remaining from the Jacobean house. The dining room has Doric pilasters and a frieze. The grand staircase is Ionic in style with a fine mural of peacocks. The walls are adorned with pictures by Whistler, Sickert and Augustus John. More 'Cloughery' can be detected in the stables and outhouses, notably a turreted cottage with a cupola, foretaste of his Portmeirion (see page 158).

Machynlleth: Royal house

⭐ Elizabethan town house with claimed royal connections

At Machynlleth, 11 miles S of Dolgellau; tourist information centre, open part year

Every self-respecting Welsh town boasts 'reputedly the oldest house in Wales', though dendrochronology has spoiled much of this fun. Machynlleth's so-called Parliament House in Maengwyn Street was heavily restored in the 20th century and historians have discredited its claim to be the seat of a Glyndwr assembly. It is probably medieval but not as old as Glyndwr, at least in its beams.

The one-time draper's shop on Heol Penrallt is older and as, 'reputedly', the resting place of Charles I is royal enough, even if the royalty is English. Its beams were felled in 1560–61 and in 1576, so this is a conventional Elizabethan town house, probably a hall with central fireplace and chimney over a merchant's store below. The entry to the latter is visible in the side elevation. The front was later extended towards the road, which is not original but admirably quaint.

The building is now the local tourist office and contains a jumble of antiquarian features. The old fireplace has a linen store cupboard next to it. A door to a rear chamber has a carved ogee transom. The roof beams and basement area are clearly original.

Legend has it that Dafydd Gam, Henry IV's reckless Welsh supporter against Glyndwr, infiltrated the Machynlleth parliament, tried to assassinate Glyndwr, was caught and imprisoned in this building in 1404. It must have been in an earlier house, but at least Gam existed, and went on to fight and die at Agincourt.

Maesmawr hall

★ Black-and-white manor house restored in the 19th century

Near Caersws, 5 miles W of Newtown; now a hotel

The hall has been a small hotel since the 1950s, its main rooms altered to form a pub and restaurant. But Maesmawr retains the layout of a Montgomeryshire manor of the unusual cruciform type, with a central chimney stack set on the diagonal to serve fireplaces in all rooms. The house was burned out in the 18th century and rebuilt, then extended by Eden Nesfield in the late 19th. The appearance is ostensibly original and looks picturesque at the end of the avenue from the Newtown road, enveloped in rambling roses and backed by woods on the banks of the Severn.

The exterior timbering is rich, the members 'close-studded' on the ground floor, rising to a local motif of baluster studding above. There are square panels with curved quadrants round the windows and in the gable. This is not repeated on the side wings. The interior is still divided into parlour and hall, with large fireplaces. The stairs retain their 18th-century balusters. It is a jolly place.

Powis castle

★★★★ Medieval house transformed by Elizabethan, Jacobean and Georgian owners

1 mile W of Welshpool; National Trust, open part year

Powis is a pocket battleship among great houses. Its rose-red walls, half as old as Wales, rise in shimmering medieval apparition over the fertile slopes of the Severn above Welshpool. Here the princes of Powys dreamed of a glory which their border geography denied them, their loyalties divided between rebellious Gwynedd and the Marches. The 13th-century prince of Powys, Gruffudd, backed Edward I against Llywelyn, and his descendants backed the English against Glyndwr, even when the Powis tenantry rose in Glyndwr's favour. Just five miles from the English border, Powis embodies Anglo-Welsh ambivalence.

In 1578 the castle passed to a junior branch of the Herberts of Wilton, who created its present mostly Tudor exterior. Catholics and Royalists, they prospered and suffered for their cause. The 1st Marquess of Powis went into exile with James II in 1688. Yet despite two centuries of imprisonment, ostracism, debt and debauchery the family contrived to improve Powis, helped by the discovery of lead on their property. The grand staircase and state rooms date from the Restoration, while the baroque gardens brought a continental swagger to soft Welsh contours.

By the 19th century the property had passed by marriage to the Clives of Shropshire, who changed their name to Herbert to merit the re-creation (for the third time) of the earldom of Powis. The castle was extensively restored by Smirke in 1815 and, in a comprehensive reversion to the Jacobean style, by Bodley at the turn of the 20th century. The castle passed to the National Trust in 1952 but the family occupy part of the house to this day.

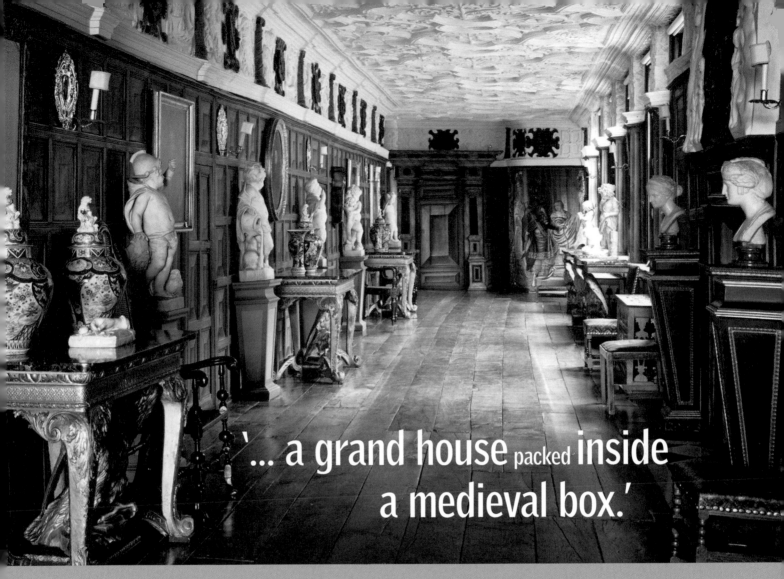

'... a grand house packed inside a medieval box.'

Above In 1578 Powis was leased to Sir Edward Herbert, of Wilton in Wiltshire; he took over complete ownership in 1587. From this date until his death in 1595, Herbert made many changes to the castle and refurbished many rooms. Later owners continued the trend and the Long Gallery is the only one to have remained as Herbert intended.

Powis is like Haddon in Derbyshire, or Alnwick in Northumberland, a grand house packed inside a medieval box. The approach is dominated by yews, descendants of ornamental shrubs that would have defined the terraces beneath the castle walls. Now they erupt like giant ice cream cones, spilling over walls and balustrades beyond all discipline.

The castle retains what must have been its Norman layout. An outer bailey is surrounded by high walls and service ranges, while a shell keep sits round an inner courtyard guarded by double drum towers. The exterior remains entirely of the 14th to 16th centuries. In sunlight its rich sandstone glows a vivid red.

The outer bailey opens over the upper Severn valley and is dominated by a spectacular statue of Fame perched perilously on a winged horse, metaphor for the family's fortunes down the ages. A curved stairway rises to the castle entrance, tucked uncomfortably between the two drum towers. The image of a pair of giant buttocks was overhead from a young tourist on my last visit.

Powis's interior is both palatial and yet domestic. There are no cavernous chambers or distant corridors. The Herberts were never rich enough to rebuild their house and had to pack what they could into the space available. Thus the entrance leads without ceremony straight to the foot of the Grand Staircase.

While modest in proportion this is elevated by a ceiling by Verrio, royal artist of Kensington Palace. It supposedly celebrates the coronation of Charles II's Queen Catherine. Below are murals of

mythological scenes by Verrio's pupil, Gerard Lanscroon, some in grisaille. These have been given back their original colours, which some may find fierce, but they respond voluptuously to the dark wood of the stairs and the baroque doorcases of the landing above. It is annoying that the National Trust will not let visitors ascend these stairs, forcing them to use the servants' access and thus detracting from the impact of a visit to Powis.

Next to the stairs on the ground floor is the dining room inserted by Bodley in place of the old medieval hall. This is Jacobean revival (1902) at its richest. Carved chimneypieces replicate ones in the Victoria and Albert museum, while family portraits by Romney and Reynolds look down from the walls. The smaller private dining room opposite was still used by the family in the 1980s.

The first floor is sensational. The state rooms were inserted in the 1660–80s, mostly by the Stuart architect, William Winde, while the family was in exile in France. They are arranged round an inner courtyard flanked on two sides by the earlier T-shaped Tudor gallery, which Winde wisely retained: Elizabethan domesticity at the service of Restoration bravura.

A lofty library contains a miniature of Lord Herbert by Isaac Oliver. The oak drawing room is mostly Bodley, rich in linenfold panelling and plaster ceiling pendants (copied from Aston Hall in Birmingham). An extraordinary Victorian fire-screen is composed of exotic stuffed birds, which cannot have survived long near any fire.

Off the gallery is the state bedroom, the most theatrical chamber in the castle. The decoration is French classical with a gilt-laden proscenium framing the great bed, secluded behind a rail to restrain

courtiers during the *leveé*. The ceiling depicts an appropriate Catholic theme, the apotheosis of the Virgin. The initials, CR, are ubiquitous, though no Stuart king ever slept here. Powis was a favourite haunt of the present Prince of Wales.

The long gallery is a charming reversion to the 16th century. Brightly lit panels and plasterwork celebrate the origins of the Herbert dynasty. Adam and Eve are invoked round the fireplace to emphasize antiquity, while the frieze is crowded with heraldry interspersed with mythical beasts. The walls are lined with Greek and Roman statuary, acquired by Clive of India, and include a sculpture of a cat playing with a snake. At the far end is a superb pietra dura table from Florence. Overseeing all is a mannerist doorcase.

After the lush interiors of the bedroom suite, the blue drawing room is calmly classical in style. It is hung with Belgian tapestries and graced with lacquerwork commodes adorned with oriental scenes. From here visitors are suddenly and unceremoniously booted down the servants' stairs, past the billiard room and out into the courtyard.

This is flanked by the old ballroom, once a picture gallery and surely too narrow for dancing. It has been divided to form the Clive of India museum, though Clive himself had nothing to do with Powis. Redesigned in 1774 in the Adam style by the Shrewsbury architect, T. F. Pritchard, it is lined with bookcases and pictures from the Clive collection. To one side is displayed the tent of the governor's great foe, Tipu Sultan. For all the splendour of the display, there is something odd in this oriental presence in the soft hills of Montgomeryshire.

Presteigne: Judge's lodgings

★★☆ Municipal museum in restored Victorian lodgings

At Presteigne, 12 miles NW of Leominster; museum, open part year

Shire halls were centres of county government and a focus of central authority. Here presided local magistrates and assize judges on tour. The buildings embraced courts, prisons, a police station and ceremonial reception rooms. They formed a governmental one-stop shop.

In Wales, and especially here in the Radnorshire border country, this meant cross-cutting loyalties between Welsh and English. Justice might have to be done through a translator. Radnorshire was one of the most secluded counties in Britain, created after the union of England and Wales in 1536. Presteigne was made the county town after a judge was murdered in the original 'capital' of the county, Rhayader.

The assize judges expected to be housed and entertained in some splendour, but since this was a charge on the town, the state of the lodgings was a source of constant complaint. The previous house at Presteigne was considered 'insufficient, inconvenient, insecure and dangerous', while the prison next door was virtually open. This led in 1826 to the rebuilding of both the courthouse and the judges lodgings, to plans by an architect named Edward Haycock.

The new building was handsome, presenting a classical façade to the street in the style of Nash. A central pilastered and pedimented block is flanked by three-bay colonnades, one for the lodgings, the other for the courthouse. Holding cells were built underneath. The new court opened in 1829, celebrated by sentencing a horse thief to death, commuted to transportation for life to Australia.

To allay the cost of the lodgings (which were irregularly used) they were sublet or used by the local militia, by magistrates or even tenanted by a court official. In 1865 they also became a territorial army mess and *de facto* town hall. The 20th-century growth of Llandrindod Wells eroded Presteigne's status and the assizes were often cancelled for want of trials, the last being held in 1970.

Rather than dispose of the building, the county restored it as Wales's best museum of municipal history. The lodgings re-create a late-Victorian domestic interior. There are not too many signs and each room is furnished as if a visiting judge was in residence, complete with portraits of county worthies. The lighting is by gas and oil, with appropriate smells, and the fittings are original, including the lavatories. There are even bottles of wine, sadly not shared with end-of-the-day visitors.

The old courtroom has been restored, as have the police cells. It retains what is claimed to be the only working gasolier left in Britain, with 18 open flame burners. The stalls and partitions are intact. But why not restore the magistrates court itself, as in Beaumaris?

Below left When the Judge's Lodgings were restored the below-stairs areas were given as much attention as the upstairs. The pantry has been furnished with contemporary Victorian pieces, including items found stored in the attics and bedrooms. **Below right** The original Victorian beds had been discarded by the time of restoration, so replacements had to be found. Where appropriate, the rooms were given new carpets copied from 19th-century designs.

Treberfydd

★★ Victorian neo-Tudor mansion of Tractarian reformer

Near Bwlch, 7 miles SE of Brecon; private house, open by arrangement

The house was built from scratch by a Hull banker, Robert Raikes, inspired in 1848 to found a centre of Anglo-Catholic Tractarianism in the Welsh hills. He had been told that such worship was in serious decline in these parts, as if Wales was a lapsed outpost of empire.

Raikes commissioned the young J. L. Pearson to design a building in a demure Victorian Tudor. A church and school were also erected on the shores of neighbouring Tal-y-llyn, the largest natural lake in south Wales. Nesfield was commissioned to lay out the gardens. Like Leighton this was a typical Victorian estate in the round, combining modern farming methods with religious rectitude. Treberfydd remains proudly in the Raikes family to this day.

The house appears from the front courtyard a characteristic early Victorian composition in the Pugin style. The façade is assymetrical, with an entrance tower, a forest of gables and chimneys in soft pink/grey stone. The windows are heavily mullioned. To the right is a second tower rising over the service courtyard, decorated with excellent gargoyles.

The interior might be that of any spacious Victorian rectory, having large rooms with even larger fireplaces, a library with its original shelving, a fine billiard room and a warm conservatory. The staircase is particularly grand with ornate finials and Raikes portraits. All is nicely cluttered. Treberfydd proves that not all Tractarian interiors need be severe.

Tretower

 Ancient castle and medieval courtyard house

At Tretower, 6½ miles NW of Abergavenny; Cadw, open part year

Tretower is the most extensive medieval house in Wales, displaying the history of the form from the Norman conquest through the Middle Ages to rebuilding in the 15th and 16th centuries. The out-houses of a modern farm have rather spoilt the setting of its adjacent castle ruin.

This ruin is remarkable (right). A motte-and-bailey was followed by a shell keep in the 12th century, within which the Norman Picard family built a hall and solar. A century later this inner courtyard was almost completely filled with a round keep, leaving the former 'shell' as an outer defensive wall. The old hall and solar were demolished where they impeded the new structure.

Each of the four floors of the new keep formed a room, with fireplaces and windows and a field of fire over the shell walls. Much of this survives, along with the post holes of bridges and links to the outer wall. The castle was defended by Lord Berkeley for the king against the Glyndwr uprising in 1403, the last time it saw active service.

A 14th-century hall house (top), some distance from the castle, was extended in the mid-15th century by Sir Roger Vaughan, a relative of the Herberts of Raglan, whose family held it into the 18th century. They gradually improved it but were never rich enough to demolish and start again. Tretower became a farm until acquired for restoration by the Brecknock Society, passing to the state in 1930.

Four ranges now enclose a courtyard entered by a gatehouse and entirely surrounded by medieval walls. The gatehouse has an impressive chamfered doorway, with a lesser postern gate to one side. A passage leads into the courtyard, with the Great Hall opposite. This is given some modest renaissance flair by the insertion of a classical doorway and large Jacobean windows, repeated on the far side of the hall facing the meadow and castle. An oriel window survives.

'Tretower is the **most extensive medieval house** in Wales ...'

Above A cross passage, about 6 feet wide, divided the main hall at Tretower from the service rooms. Today the walls of these rooms have gone and the passage opens onto an empty space. In the 15th century there would have been four service rooms here, where food was prepared before being taken into either the main hall or the retainers' mess hall.

The interior of the main hall, built by Vaughan to replace the earlier one in the north range, is spacious, divided by screens rising to the roof with trefoil and quatrefoil openings. At one end is the solar with latrines built into the wall and a kitchen beyond, at the other are service rooms and a servants' mess. That this arrangement should have survived across the centuries is remarkable.

In the 1460s Vaughan divided the rest of the building into residential apartments on the first floor. This involved inserting a floor in what had been the old 14th-century hall in the north range, with a new upper hall complete with fireplace and partitions for bedrooms. This suggests that the range was for a separate family, or at least for Vaughan's much extended one. The long upper chamber is a magnificent medieval room, rich in woodwork. Restoration has revealed early leaf and 'teardrop' painted decoration on the rendered partitions. Outside, a balcony runs round two sides of the courtyard and offers sheltered access to the upstairs rooms under the roof eaves. It is all most picturesque.

Tretower demonstrates the conundrum of historic house presentation. The exposure of the service end of the hall, with open floors and removed walls, conveys no sense either of what the old house looked like or of a modern reinstatement. It is as if an archaeologist had enjoyed himself tearing the place apart and gone off to write a thesis. The residential quarters are completely bare, despite being fully roofed and thus useable. This place needs urgent attention.

Trewern hall

★ Jacobean black-and-white house with Elizabethan origins

4 miles NE of Welshpool; private house, open part year

Mid Wales must once have been thick with houses such as Trewern. Of those that survive, few are accessible and Trewern is the more precious. It sits as it has for centuries, a piano keyboard of black and white rising to four patterned gables. The original house has been dated to the 1560s, but this probably consisted of the present kitchen wing, to which the main house was a cross wing.

Dating is confused by the richness of the later alteration, undertaken by Robert Francis with a date of 1610 over the porch. This was clearly designed to reflect a Jacobean desire for symmetry, no easy thing in a medieval hall house. The later work includes a jettied upper storey carrying excellent if battered carvings of heads and vegetation in the corbels. The gable brickwork is herringbone.

The house was again altered in the Victorian era, with the aim of creating a grander, less 'yeoman', house. The present owner, Murray Chapman, whose family acquired the property in 1918, has laboured hard to reinstate the previous Jacobean form. This has involved drastic intervention, notably modern windows and other woodwork, which inevitably detracts from the appearance of antiquity. But all wooden houses need renewal, and all look old in time.

Glossary

The aim in this book has been to avoid terms not familiar to the lay person. However, some specialist terms in common use in architectural circles may have crept in, for which the following may be helpful.

acanthus – pattern of an exotic Mediterranean flower with large leaves used in classical decoration.

anthemion – a honeysuckle flower pattern used in classical decoration.

Artisan Mannerist – buildings created by masons using pattern books (rather than architects) in the period c.1615–75. Mannerism originated in 16th-century Italy and was characterised by Classical elements used in unusual ways. It was taken up in the Low Countries, then spread to England.

ashlar – block of masonry fashioned into a wall, either load-bearing or to cover brick.

bailey, inner and outer – a fortified enclosure, usually moated and surrounded by a curtain wall, containing a motte (mound) with a keep on top. Walls are topped by battlements, with crenellations which protected defenders from arrows, and machicolations, or floor openings, through which attackers could be fired down on.

baluster – upright post supporting the handrail on stairs.

bargeboard – wooden board protecting the eaves of a roof.

bay – a space of wall between any vertical element, such as an upright beam, pillar or a division into a window or door.

bay window – window projecting out from a flat wall, either canted if the sides are straight, or bowed if curved.

bolection mould – moulding concealing the join of vertical and horizontal surfaces, shaped like an S in cross-section.

Boulle – elaborate inlay work on the surface of furniture, customary in 17th and 18th-century French work.

bow – see bay window

canted – see bay window

cartouche – frame for a picture or statue, often oval and surrounded by a scroll.

caryatid – a column in the shape of a draped female figure.

casements – see sashes

castle of enclosure – a form of early medieval castle in which individual buildings are enclosed within a curtain wall, in contrast to later medieval castles that consisted of a tower with subsidiary buildings in a courtyard to front or rear.

chinoiserie – a style of Rococo with Chinese motifs, often linked with Gothick.

coffering – a ceiling composed of beams enclosing sunken square or round panels.

collars – see roof timbers

corbel – a stone or wood projection in a wall that supports a beam, statue or sill.

cornice – (1) a ledge or projecting upper part of a classical entablature. (2) Moulding at the top of a wall concealing the join with the ceiling.

cottage ornée – late-Georgian/Victorian picturesque cottage, usually with thatched roof and Gothic windows.

crenellation – see bailey

crocket – Gothic decorative device, usually a cusp or curling leaf, at regular intervals on outer edges of spires, pinnacles and gables

cromlech – a prehistoric monument of standing stones

cruck – a simple structure of two, usually curved, trunks of wood formed into an inverted V which support the walls and roof of a medieval house.

curtain wall – in castle-building, a wall constructed between defensive projections such as bastions.

dentil – one of a series of small square blocks along the base of a cornice

dorter – a sleeping room or dormitory, especially in a college or monastery.

dressing – a general term for finishings; stone is dressed to either a smooth or ornamental surface.

enfilade – a line of rooms in sequence along one side of a house, usually with interconnecting doors.

entablature – a feature of classical architecture comprising everything above column height, formally composed of architrave, frieze and cornice.

flatwork – decorative plaster or woodwork in low relief.

frontispiece – a decorative bay above a doorway in a Tudor or Jacobean building, customarily composed of Renaissance motifs.

gable – the triangular end of a double-pitched roof, sometimes with stepped or scrolled (Dutch) sides.

garderobe – privy or lavatory, usually discharging into a ditch or moat outside a medieval house.

Great Chamber – see solar

grisaille – monochrome painting, usually a mural and in shades of grey.

grotesque – decorative wall motif of human figures, as found in Roman grottoes.

half-timbering – term for timber-framed house derived from the practice of splitting logs in half to provide beams.

hipped roof – a roof with a sloping end instead of an end gable.

Ho-Ho bird – chinoiserie motif associated with 18th-century Rococo style.

jetty or jettied floor – upper floor extended, or oversailed, beyond the lower one to give more space upstairs and protect lower walls from adverse weather. Jettying also uses the downward thrust of the upper walls to form a cantilever, preventing internal ceiling beams from bowing.

keep – see bailey

king post – see roof timbers

lierne – a reinforcing rib used in Gothic vaulting

linenfold – a pattern on wall panels imitating folded linen.

louvre – a covered turret above a medieval hall that allowed smoke to escape.

machicolation – see bailey

mannerism – see Artisan Mannerist

mansard – a roof with two separate pitches of slope.

motte – see bailey

mullion – central divider of window, made of metal or stone.

oversail – see jetty

oriel – an upper window projecting from a wall, sometimes (incorrectly) used to indicate a tall medieval window lighting the dais end of the Great Hall.

Palladian – a style of classical architecture, formal and refined outside, often lavish inside, named after Italian architect, Andrea Palladio (1508–80). Moving spirit behind most English classical designers, especially Inigo Jones and, later, Lord Burlington, William Kent and the early Georgians.

parlour – see solar

piano nobile – the main ceremonial floor of a classical building, sitting on the basement or 'rustic' lower floor.

pier-glass – a wall mirror supported by a small table, bracket or console.

pietra dura – literally 'hard stone'; a decorative inlay using highly polished stones such as marble, jasper and porphyry

pilaster – a flat column projecting only slightly from a wall.

pointing – mortar or cement used to seal between bricks.

porte-cochère – a grand porch with a driveway through it, allowing passengers to alight from carriages under cover.

prodigy house – a large, ostentatious house of the Elizabethan/Jacobean period.

putti – unwinged sculptures of chubby boys found in Classical and Baroque decoration.

queen post – see roof timbers

quoins – dressed corner stones.

render – a covering of stucco, cement or limewash on the outside of a building.

Rococo – the final phase of Baroque style in the 18th century, typified by refined painted and plaster decoration, often asymmetrical and with figures.

roof timbers – a tie-beam runs horizontally across the roof space; a king post rises vertically from the tie beam to the apex of the roof; queen posts rise not to the apex but to subsidiary beams known as collars; wind-braces strengthen the roof rafters.

rustic – a name given in Palladian architecture to the lower floor or basement, beneath the piano nobile.

rustication – treatment of ashlar by deep-cutting joints so they look stronger or cruder.

sashes – windows opening by rising on sash ropes or cords, as opposed to casements which open on side hinges.

scagliola – composition of artificial stone that imitates appearance of grained marble.

screens passage – accessed from the main door of a medieval building and built into one end of a Great Hall to shield it from draughts. Door ors arches lead from the passage into the hall on one side and kitchens on other. Above is usually a minstrels' gallery.

Serlian – motifs derived from pattern books of the Italian Renaissance architect, Sebastiano Serlio (1475–1554).

sgraffito – plaster decoration scratched to reveal another colour beneath.

solar – the upstairs room at the family end of a medieval hall, originally above an undercroft or parlour. Originally accessed by ladder or spiral stairs, it was usually replaced by a Great Chamber in the Tudor era.

strapwork – strap or ribbon-like decorative scrolls in Elizabethan and Jacobean design.

stucco – plaster, usually protective, covering for brick, sometimes fashioned to look like stone.

studding – vertical timbers laid close to each other to strengthen the wall. Close-studding tends to indicate wealth.

tie-beam – see roof timbers

undercroft – a vaulted room or crypt beneath a building, partly or wholly underground

vault – an arched ceiling, usually of stone

Venetian window – Palladian window composed of three components, the centre one arched.

wind-braces – see roof timbers

Simon Jenkins' sources

The best guides to any house are the people who occupy it. They have felt its walls and sensed its seasons. They stand witness to its ghosts, real and imagined, and have thus become part of its history. As a substitute, guidebooks vary widely from the academic to the plain childish. The best are published by English Heritage and Cadw, erudite and enjoyable. National Trust guidebooks are at last moving from the scholarly to the accessible, and the Trust's compendium *Guide*, by Lydia Greeves and Michael Trinick, is excellent.

My selection of properties featured in *DISCOVER BRITAIN'S HISTORIC HOUSES* derives from numerous sources. These include Hudson's *Historic Houses and Gardens*, supplemented by *Museums and Galleries* published by Tomorrow's Guides. The Historic Houses Association website is another invaluable source. Of recent house surveys, the best are John Julius Norwich's *Architecture of Southern England* (1985), John Martin Robinson's *Architecture of Northern England* (1986) and Hugh Montgomery-Massingberd's *Great Houses of England and Wales* (2000). Nigel Nicolson's *Great Houses of Britain* (1978) describes the most prominent. Their lists are not exhaustive and include houses not open to the public. Behind them stands Nikolaus Pevsner's massive 'Buildings of England' series, which deals with houses more generously (with plans) in the newer revised editions.

On English domestic architecture, the classics are hard to beat. They include Olive Cook's *The English House Through Seven Centuries* (1968), Alec Clifton-Taylor's *The Pattern of English Building* (1972), Hugh Braun's *Old English Houses* (1962), Sacheverell Sitwell's *British Architects and Craftsmen* (1964) and Plantagenet Somerset Fry's *Castles of Britain and Ireland* (1980).

On specific periods the best are Mark Girouard's *Robert Smythson and the English Country House* (1983), Giles Worsley's *Classical Architecture in England* (1995), Kerry Downes's *English Baroque Architecture* (1966) and Girouard's *The Victorian Country House* (1971). Joe Mordaunt Crook takes a lively look at the Victorian battle of the styles in *The Dilemma of Style* (1989). Jeremy Musson describes the manorial revival in *The English Manor House* (1999) and Gavin Stamp takes a wider look at the same period in *The English House 1860–1914* (1986). *Edwardian Architecture*, edited by Alastair Service (1975), brings the story into the 20th century and Clive Aslet's *The Last Country Houses* (1982) almost completes it.

On social history, Girouard's *Life in the English Country House* (1978) is incomparable. *Creating Paradise* (2000) by Richard Wilson and Alan Mackley sets the house in its economic context. So does Mordaunt Crook's *The Rise of the Nouveaux Riches* (1999) and David Cannadine's *The Decline and Fall of the British Aristocracy* (1990). Adrian Tinniswood offers a fascinating insight in his *History of Country House Visiting* (1989). The desperate post-war bid to save houses is described in Marcus Binney's *Our Vanishing Heritage* (1984) and John Cornforth's *The Country Houses of England 1948–1998* (1998). Peter Mandler covers the same period in his scholarly *The Fall and Rise of the Stately Home* (1997).

Biographies of architects are too legion to list but Howard Colvin's *Biographical Dictionary of British Architects* (1978) was my bible over disputed dates and attributions. Of a more personal character is James Lees-Milne's delightful account of the National Trust's early acquisitions in *People and Places* (1992). Houses in distress are visited in John Harris's *No Voice from the Hall* (1998). *Writers and their Houses* (1993) is a first-class collection of essays, edited by Kate Marsh.

I am indebted to the many architectural commentaries in *Country Life*, champion of the historic buildings cause for over a century. I do not believe I could have found a thousand houses for my list were it not for its progenitors, Edward Hudson and Christopher Hussey, and their many successors.

Contact details

Note: Readers are advised to check opening times before visiting, either via the websites and addresses below or in Hudson's *Historic Houses & Gardens*, the annual guide to castles, houses and heritage sites open to the public. Houses sited close to the border of a neighbouring county may have that county given as their postal address.

Abbey-cwm-Hir – Abbey-cwm-Hir, Powys, LD1 6PH
www.abbeycwmhir.com Tel 01597 851727 Open for pre-booked tours
Abercamlais – Brecon, Powys, LD3 8EY www.abercamlais.co.uk
Tel 01874 636206 Open by appointment in Apr–Oct
Aberystwyth: Old College – King Street, Aberystwyth, Ceredigion, SY23 2AX Tel 01970 623111 Contact the university for access information
Beaumaris Castle – Beaumaris, Anglesey, LL58 8AP
www.cadw.wales.gov.uk Tel 01248 810361 Open all year, daily 9.30am–4pm (from 11am on Sun in Nov–Mar, to 5pm in Apr–May & Oct, to 6pm in Jun–Sep)
Beaumaris: Old Gaol – Steeple Lane, Beaumaris, Anglesey. LL58 8EP
www.angleseyheritage.org Tel 01248 810921 Open Easter–Sep, daily 10.30am–5pm
Blaenavon Ironworks – Nr Brecon Beacons National Park, Blaenavon, Gwent www.cadw.wales.gov.uk Tel 01495 792615 Open Apr–Oct, daily 9.30am–4.30pm (from 10am on Sat–Sun)
Bodelwyddan – Bodelwyddan, Denbighshire, LL18 5YA
www.bodelwyddan-castle.co.uk Tel 01745 584060 Open all year, Sat–Thur (Thur & Sat–Sun only in Nov–Easter) 10.30am–5pm (to 4pm in Nov–Easter)
Bodrhydden Hall – Rhuddlan, Denbighshire, LL18 5SB
www.bodrhyddan.co.uk Tel 01745 590414 Open Jun–Sep, Tue & Thur 2–5.30pm
Bodysgallen Hall Hotel – Llandudno, LL30 1RS www.bodysgallen.com Tel 01492 584466
Bryn Bras Castle – Llanrug, Caernarfon, Gwynedd, LL55 4RE
www.brynbrascastle.co.uk Tel 01286 870210 Open by appointment only (NB no children)
Caernarfon Castle – Castle Ditch, Caernarfon, LL55 2AY
www.cadw.wales.gov.uk Tel 01286 677617 Open all year, daily 9.30am–4pm (from 11am on Sun in Nov–Mar, to 5pm in Apr–May & Oct, to 6pm in Jun–Sep)
Caerphilly Castle – Caerphilly, CF8 1JL www.cadw.wales.gov.uk
Tel 029 2088 3143 Open all year, daily 9.30am–4pm (from 11am on Sun in Nov–Mar, to 5pm in Apr–May & Oct, to 6pm in Jun–Sep)
Caldicot Castle – Church Road, Caldicot, Monmouthshire, NP26 4HU
www.caldicotcastle.co.uk Tel 01291 420241 Open Apr–Sep, daily 11am–5pm
Cardiff Castle – Castle Street, Cardiff, CF10 3RB www.cardiffcastle.com
Tel 029 2087 8100 Open all year, daily 9.30am–5pm (to 6pm in Mar–Oct)
Carew Castle – Carew, Nr Tenby, Pembrokeshire, SA70 8SL
www.carewcastle.com Tel 01646 651782 Open all year, daily 10am–5pm (11am–3pm in Nov–Easter)
Carreg Cennen Castle – Tir-y-Castel Farm, Llandeilo, Carmarthenshire
www.cadw.wales.gov.uk Tel 01558 822291 Open all year daily 9.30am–6.30pm (to 4pm in Nov–Mar)
Castell Coch – Tongwynlais, Cardiff, CF4 7JS www.cadw.wales.gov.uk
Tel 029 2081 0101 Open all year, daily 9.30am–4pm (from 11am on Sun in Nov–Mar, to 5pm in Apr–May & Oct, to 6pm in Jun–Sep)
Chepstow Castle – Chepstow, Gwent www.cadw.wales.gov.uk
Tel 01292 624065 Open all year, daily 9.30am–4pm (from 11am on Sun in Nov–Mar, to 5pm in Apr–May & Oct, to 6pm in Jun–Sep)
Chirk – Chirk, Wrexham, LL14 5AF www.nationaltrust.org.uk
Tel 01691 777701 Open early Feb–mid-Dec, Wed–Sun (also Tue in Jul–Aug, Sat–Sun only in early–mid-Feb & early–mid-Dec) 11am–4pm (to 5pm in mid-Mar–late Sep & early–mid-Dec)
Cilgerran Castle – Cardigan, Dyfed www.cadw.wales.gov.uk
Tel 01239 615007 Open all year, daily 9.30am–6pm (to 5pm in Oct and to 4pm in Nov–Mar)
Clytha Castle – Contact the Landmark Trust: www.landmarktrust.org.uk
Tel 01628 825925

Cochwillan Old Hall – Tal-y-Bont, Bangor, Gwynedd, LL57 3AZ
Tel 01248 355853 Open by appointment
Conwy Castle – Rose Hill Street, Conwy, LL32 8AY
www.cadw.wales.gov.uk Tel 01492 592358 Open all year, daily 9.30am–4pm (from 11am on Sun in Nov–Mar, to 5pm in Apr–May & Oct, to 6pm in Jun–Sep)
Conwy: Aberconwy House – Castle Street, Conwy, LL32 8AY
www.nationaltrust.org.uk Tel 01492 592246 Open late Mar–early Nov, Wed–Mon 11am–5pm
Conwy: Plas Mawr – High Street, Conwy, LL32 8EF
www.cadw.wales.gov.uk Tel 01492 580167 Open all year, Tue–Sun & BH Mon 9.30am–5pm (to 6pm in Jun–Aug, to 4pm in Oct)
Craig-y-nos Castle – Brecon Road, Pen-y-cae, Powys, SA9 1GL
www.craigynoscastle.com Tel 01639 731167 or 730205
Cresselly – Kilgetty, Pembrokeshire, SA68 0SP www.cresselly.org.uk
Tel 01646 687045 Open early Jun–mid-July, Mon–Fri 10am–1pm for guided tours on the hour (NB: no children under 12)
Cyfarthfa Castle – Brecon Road, Merthyr Tydfil, Mid Glamorgan, CF47 8RE www.museums.merthyr.gov.uk Tel 01685 723112 Open all year, daily (closed Mon in Oct–Mar) 10am–4pm (from 12pm on Sun in Oct–Mar, to 5.30pm in Apr–Sep)
Din Lligwy – Nr Moelfre, Anglesey (OS ref: SH 497 861)
www.cadw.wales.gov.uk Open all year, daily at any reasonable time
Dinefwr – Newton House, Dinefwr Park, Llandeilo, Carmarthenshire, SA19 6RT www.nationaltrust.org.uk Tel 01558 824512
Open mid-Mar–late Dec, daily (Fri–Sun in early Nov–late Dec) 11am–5pm
Dinorwic Quarry Hospital – Padarn Country Park, Llanberis, Gwynedd, LL55 4TY Tel 01286 870892 Open Easter school holidays, Spring BH–mid-Sep & Oct half term, daily 9am–5pm; park open all year
Dolwyddelan Castle – Blaenau Ffestiniog, Gywnedd
www.cadw.wales.gov.uk Tel 01690 750366 Open all year, daily 10am–6pm (to 4pm on Sun & Oct–Mar)
Erddig – Wrexham, LL13 0YT www.nationaltrust.org.uk
Tel 01978 315151/355314 Open mid-Mar–late Dec, Sat–Wed (also Thur in Jul–Aug, Sat–Sun only in early Nov–late Dec) 12–4pm (to 5pm in early Apr–late Sep)
Fonmon Castle – Fonmon, Barry, Vale of Glamorgan, CF62 3ZN
Tel 01446 710206 Open Apr–Sep, Tue–Wed 2–5pm
Greenfield: Pentre Farmhouse – Abbey Farm Museum, Greenfield Valley Heritage Park, Greenfield, Holywell, Flintshire, H8 7GH
www.greenfieldvalley.com Tel 01352 714172 Open late Mar–early Nov, daily 10am–4.30pm
Gregynog Hall – University of Wales, Tregynon, Nr Newtown, Powys, SY16 3PW www.wales.ac.uk/gregynog Tel 01686 650224 Contact for access information
Gwrych Castle – Abergele is located on the A547, between Abergele and Llanddulas, not far from the A55 Contact the Gwrych Castle Preservation Trust for further information: 7 Clive Avenue, Prestatyn, Denbighshire, LL19 7BL www.gwrychtrust.co.uk
Gwydir Castle – Llanrwst, Gwynedd, LL26 0PN www.gwydircastle.co.uk
Tel 01492 641687 Open Mar–Oct, Tue–Fri & Sun (also Mon & Sat on BH weekends) 10am–4pm
Hafodunos Hall – Llangernyw, Conwy, Denbighshire, LL22 8TY
www.hafodunos-hall.co.uk The property is currently for sale: contact Walker Singleton Asset Management of Halifax for further information
Harlech Castle – Castle Square, Harlech, LL46 2YH
www.cadw.wales.gov.uk Tel 01766 780552 Open all year, daily 9.30am–4pm (from 11am on Sun in Nov–Mar, to 5pm in Apr–May & Oct, to 6pm in Jun–Sep)
Hartsheath Estate – Pontblyddyn, Mold, Flintshire Tel 01352 770204
Open by arrangement on 1st, 3rd & 5th Wed in every month, 2–5pm
Hay Castle – Hay-on-Wye, Hereford, HR3 5AJ
www.richardbooth.demon.co.uk/haycastle.htm Tel 01497 820503
Open all year, daily 9.30am–6pm (9am–5.30pm in late Oct–late Mar)
Iscoyd Park – Nr Whitchurch, Shropshire, SY13 3AT Open by written appointment only; contact Mr Godsal

Kidwelly Castle – Kidwelly, West Glamorgan, SA17 5BG
www.cadw.wales.gov.uk Tel 01554 890104 Open all year, daily 9.30am–4pm (from 11am on Sun in Nov–Mar, to 5pm in Apr–May & Oct, to 6pm in Jun–Sep)

Kinmel Park – Abergele, Conwy LL22 9DA www.kinmel-estate.co.uk Tel 01745 826263 Only exterior can by viewed; open by arrangement

Lampeter: St David's College – College Street, Lampeter, Ceredigion, SA48 7ED www.lamp.ac.uk Tel 01570 422351 Contact the university for access information

Laugharne Castle – King Street, Laugharne, SA33 4SA
www.cadw.wales.gov.uk Tel 01994 427906 Open Apr–Sep, daily 10am–5pm

Laugharne: Dylan Thomas House – Dylan's Walk, Laugharne, SA33 4SD www.dylanthomasboathouse.com Tel 01994 427420
Open all year, daily 10am–5.30pm (10.30am–3.30pm in Nov–Apr)

Llancaiach Fawr – Nelson, Treharris, CF46 6ER Tel 01443 412248
Open all year, daily (closed Mon in Nov–Feb) 10am–5pm

Llanerchaeron – Cilau Aeron, Aberaeron, Ceredigion, SA49 8DG
www.nationaltrust.org.uk Tel 01545 570200/573024 Open mid-Mar–early Nov, Wed–Sun & BH Mon (also Tue in late Jun–late Aug)

Llanfyllin: The Council House – High Street, Llanfyllin, Powys Tel 01691 648244 Contact the owners, Mr & Mrs Danby, for access information

Llanrwst Almshouses – Church Street, Llanrwst, LL26 OLE
www.conwy.gov.uk Tel 01492 642550 Open all year, Tue–Sun 10.30am–3.30pm (from 12pm on Sat–Sun)

Llanvihangel Court – Nr Abergavenny, Monmouthshire, NP7 8DH
www.llanvihangel-court.co.uk Tel 01873 890217 Open on certain days in May & Aug; contact for further information

Lloyd George's Boyhood Home – Llanystumdwy, Criccieth, Gwynedd, LL52 0SH Tel 01766 522071 Open Easter & May–Sep, Mon–Fri & BH weekends (and Sat in Jun, daily in Jul–Sep) 10.30am–5pm (11am–4pm in Oct)

Machynlleth: Royal House – Penrallt St, Machynlleth, Powys, SY20 8AG Tel 01654 702401 The building is now a Tourist Information Centre and open during normal hours

Maesmawr Hall Hotel – Caersws, Powys, SY17 5SF
www.maesmawr.co.uk Tel 01686 688255

Manorbier Castle – Manorbier, Tenby, Pembrokeshire, SA70 7TB
www.manorbiercastle.co.uk Tel 01834 871394 Open Easter–Sep, daily 10.30am–5.30pm

Margam Castle – Margam Country Park, Margam, Port Talbot, SA13 2TJ
www.npt.gov.uk Tel 01639 881635 Open all year, daily 10am–4.30pm (to 5pm in Apr–Sep, from 1pm on Mon–Tue in Oct–Mar)

Nanteos Mansion – Rhydyfelin, Aberystwyth, Ceredigion SY23 4LU
www.nanteos.co.uk Tel 01970 624363 Contact for access information

Old Beaupre Castle – St Hilary, Cowbridge, Vale of Galmorgan
www.cadw.wales.gov.uk 029 2082 6185 Open all year, daily at any reasonable time

Oxwich Castle – Oxwich Castle Farm, Oxwich, SA3 1NG
www.cadw.wales.gov.uk Tel 01792 390359 Open Apr–Sep, daily 10am–5pm

Pembroke Castle – Pembroke, SA71 4LA www.pembrokecastle.co.uk
Tel 01646 681510 Open all year, daily 10am–4pm (from 9.30am & to 6pm in Apr–Sep, to 5pm in Mar & Oct)

Pennal: Cefn Caer – Pennal, Machynlleth, Powys, SY20 9JX
www.cefncaer.co.uk Tel 01654 791230 Open by appointment

Penrhyn Castle – Bangor, LL57 4HN www.nationaltrust.org.uk
Tel 01248 353084 Open late Mar–early Nov, Wed–Mon 12–5pm

Picton Castle – Haverfordwest, Pembrokeshire, SA62 4AS
www.pictoncastle.co.uk Tel 01437 751326 Open Apr–Sep , Tue–Sun & BH Mon 12–4pm for guided tours only

Plas Newydd – Llanfairpwll, Anglesey, LL61 6DQ www.nationaltrust.org.uk
Tel 01248 714795 or 715272 Open early Mar–late Oct, Sat–Wed (also Good Fri) 12–5pm (to 4pm in early–mid-Mar)

Plas Newydd – Hill Street, Llangollen, Denbighshire, LL20 8AW
Tel 01978 861314 Open Apr–Oct, daily 10am–5pm

Plas Teg – Mold Road, Pontblyddyn, Mold, Flintshire, CH7 4HN
www.plasteg.co.uk Tel 01352 771335 Open all year, Sun 2–5pm

Plas yn Rhiw – Rhiw, Pwllheli, LL53 8AB www.nationaltrust.org.uk
Tel 01758 780219 Open mid-Mar–early Nov, Thur–Mon (also Wed in Jul–Aug, Thur–Sun in mid-Mar–late Apr & early Oct–early Nov) 12–5pm (to 4pm in early Oct–early Nov)

Portmeirion – Portmeirion, Gwynedd, LL48 6ET
www.portmeirion-village.com Tel 01766 770000 Open all year, daily 9.30am–5.30pm

Powis Castle – Nr Welshpool, SY21 8RF www.nationaltrust.org.uk
Tel 01938 551929/551944 Open mid-Mar–early Nov, Thur–Mon (also Wed in Jul–Aug) 1–5pm (to 4pm in late Sep–early Nov)

Presteigne: Judge's Lodgings – Broad Street, Presteigne, Powys, LD8 2AD www.judgeslodging.org.uk Tel 01544 260650 Open early Mar–late Dec, Wed–Sun (daily in Mar–Oct) 10am–4pm (to 5pm in Mar–Oct)

Raglan Castle – Raglan, NP5 2BT www.cadw.wales.gov.uk
Tel 01291 690228 Open all year, daily 9.30am–4pm (from 11am on Sun in Nov–Mar, to 5pm in Apr–May & Oct, to 6pm in Jun–Sep)

Ruthin Castle Hotel – Castle Street, Ruthin, Denbighshire, LL15 2NU
www.ruthincastle.co.uk Tel 01824 702664

Ruthin: Nantclwyd House – Castle Street, Ruthin, Denbighshire, LL15 1DP www.denbighshire.gov.uk Tel 01824 709822 Open Apr–Sep, Fri–Sun 10–5pm

St Davids: Bishop's Palace – The Close, St Davids, Pembrokeshire, SA62 6PE www.cadw.wales.gov.uk Tel 01437 720517 Open all year, daily 9.30am–4pm (from 11am on Sun in Nov–Mar, to 5pm in Apr–May & Oct, to 6pm in Jun–Sep)

St Donat's Castle – Atlantic College, Llantwit Major, Glamorgan, CF61 1WF www.atlanticcollege.org Tel 01446 799000 Contact the college for access information

St Fagans National History Museum: Rhyd-y-Car Iron Worker's Houses and St Fagans Castle – St Fagans, Cardiff, CF5 6XB
www.museumwales.ac.uk/en/stfagans/ Tel 029 2057 3500 Open all year, daily 10am–5pm

Soughton Hall Hotel – Northop, Flintshire CH7 6AB
www.soughtonhall.co.uk Telephone: 01352 840811

Tenby: Merchant's House – Quay Hill, Tenby, Pembrokeshire SA70 7BX
www.nationaltrust.org.uk Tel 01834 842279 late Mar–early Nov, Sun–Fri (also Sat on BH weekends) 11am–5pm

Tower – Nercwys, Mold, Flintshire, CH7 4EW www.towerwales.co.uk
Tel 01352 700220 Open on certain days in May & Aug; contact for further information

Treberfydd – Bwlch, Powys, LD3 7PX www.treberfydd.net
Tel 01874 730205 Open in Aug for pre-booked tours

Tredegar House – Newport, NP1 9YW
www.newport.gov.uk/tredegarhouse Tel 01633 815880 Open Easter–Sep, Wed–Sun & BHs 11.30am–4pm

Treowen – Wonastow, Nr Monmouth, NP25 4DL www.treowen.co.uk
Tel 01600 712031 Open May–Jun & Aug–Sep, Fri 10am–4pm (also open on certain weekends, contact for information)

Tretower Court – Tretower, Crickhowell, NP8 2RF
www.cadw.wales.gov.uk Tel 01874 730279 Open Mar–Oct, Tue–Sun 10am–4pm (to 5pm in Apr–Sep)

Trevor Hall – Trevor Hall Road, Garth, Llangollen, Denbighshire, LL20 7UP
www.trevorhall.com Tel 01978 810505 Contact for access information

Trewern Hall – Trewern, Welshpool, Powys, SY21 8DT Tel 01938 570243
Open late Apr–late May, Mon–Fri 2–5pm

Ty Hyll – Capel Curig, Conwy, LL24 0DS www.snowdonia-society.org.uk
Tel 01690 720287 Open all year, Mon–Fri (daily Easter–Oct) 9.30am–5pm

Ty Mawr – Penmachno, Betws-y-Coed, Conwy, LL25 0HJ
www.nationaltrust.org.uk Tel 01690 760213 Open mid-Mar–early Nov, Thur–Sun, 12–5pm (to 4pm in early Oct–early Nov)

Usk Castle – Usk, Monmouthshire, NP5 1SD www.uskcastle.com
Tel 01291 672563 Ruins open all year daily, 11am–5pm; Castle House open Jun, daily 2–5pm

Weobley Castle – Weobley Castle Farm, Llanrhidian, SA3 1HB
www.cadw.wales.gov.uk Tel 01792 390012 Open all year, daily 9.30am–6pm (to 5pm in Nov–Mar)

Wern Isaf – Penmaen Park, Llanfairfechan, LL33 0RN Tel 01248 680437
Open early–late Mar, Wed–Mon 1–4pm

White Castle – Llantillio Crossenny, Gwent www.cadw.wales.gov.uk
Tel 01600 780380 Open all year, daily 10am–4pm (only staffed Apr–Sep, Wed–Sun)

Index

Main entries for houses are in **bold**

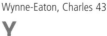

T=top TL=top left TR=top right B=bottom BL=bottom left BR=bottom right
L=left R=right C=centre CL=centre left CR=centre right

Front Cover Country Life/Paul Barker (Plas Teg, view into the Hall)
Back Cover Dick Wheelock (Treowen, north elevation in snow) **Endpapers** The
National Trust/Barry Hamilton (Based on a piece of early 18th century wallpaper
found in the attic at Erddig) **1** John Parker (Tredegar House, 18th century tiles,
 Best Chamber fireplace) **2-3** The National Trust/Nick Meers (Plas Newydd, east front
with the Menai Straits and Snowdonia in the background) **4-8** European Map
Graphics Ltd. **11** © Reader's Digest/Illustration by Hardlines Ltd **12** RIBA Library
Photographs Collection **14-15** CADW. Crown Copyright **16** The Photolibrary
Wales/David Angel **17-19** John Parker **20 TL** The National Trust/Christopher
Gallagher **20-21 T** The National Trust/Andreas von Einsiedel **B** The National
Trust/Matthew Antrobus **21 R** The National Trust/Andreas von Einsiedel **22** The
National Trust/Andreas von Einsiedel **23** The National Trust/Rupert Truman
24-26 The National Trust/Andreas von Einsiedal **27** John Parker **28-29** Country
Life/Paul Barker **30** John Parker **31** Dan Jones Photography **32** Reproduced by
permission of the Clwyd-Powys Archaeological Trust/(1321-016) **33-36** John Parker
37-39 Country Life/Paul Barker **40** Courtesy of Ruthin Castle **41** John Parker
42 Courtesy of Soughton Hall **43** Courtesy of Tower **44-45** Courtesy of Trevor Hall
46-47 CADW. Crown Copyright **48-49** Janet Baxter **49 T** Janet Baxter
B Aberystwyth University **50-51** Pembrokeshire Coast National Park Authority
52 CADW. Crown Copyright **53** The National Trust/Joe Cornish **54 T** John Parker
55-56 The National Trust/John Hammond **57** CADW. Crown Copyright **58** University
of Wales Lampeter **59** CADW. Crown Copyright **60** David Lyons **61 T** Ralph
Carpenter, Carmarthenshire County Council. **B** Mary Evans Picture Library
62 Country Life/Paul Barker **63** The National Trust/Andreas von Einsiedel
64-65 The Photolibrary Wales/Chris Warren **66-71** John Parker **72** CADW. Crown
Copyright **73 L** The National Trust/John Heseltine **R** The National Trust/Erik Pelham
74-75 The Photolibrary Wales/Glyn Evans **76-77** CADW. Crown Copyright
78-81 John Parker **82-85** CADW. Crown Copyright **86** David Lyons
88-89 John Parker **90-91** © Caerphilly County Borough Council **91** John Parker
92-93 T The Photolibrary Wales/Mark Mumford **B** Alison Lloyd **94** Mick Sharp and
Jean Williamson **95** CADW. Crown Copyright **96** James Mendelssohn **97** © National
Museum Wales **98 T** Collections/McQuillan & Brown **B** © National Museum Wales
99-103 CADW. Crown Copyright **104-105** John Parker/(with thanks to Caldicot
Castle and Country Park, Monmouthshire County Council) **105** John Parker
106-107 CADW. Crown Copyright **108** The Landmark Trust **109-110** John Parker
111 www.britainonview.com **112 L** The Photolibrary Wales/Brian Griffiths **R** CADW.
Crown Copyright **113-116** John Parker **117** Dick Wheelock **118-119** John Parker
120-123 CADW. Crown Copyright **124 L** Mick Sharp and Jean Williamson
124-125 John Parker **126** www.historichousehotels.com **127-128** John Parker
129-130 CADW. Crown Copyright **131** John Parker **132-133** CADW. Crown
Copyright **134** The National Trust/Matthew Antrobus **135-137** CADW. Crown
Copyright **138** Mick Sharp and Jean Williamson **138-139** Gerallt Llewelyn
140-141 CADW. Crown Copyright **141 R** The Bridgeman Art Library/Private
collection **142-145** John Parker **146** CADW. Crown Copyright **147-148** John Parker
149 Elfyn Rowlands **150** The National Trust/Geoff Morgan **151-153** The National
Trust/Andreas von Einsiedel **154 T** The National Trust/Andreas von Einsiedel
154-155 The National Trust/Nick Meers **156** The National Trust/Andreas von
Einsiedel/© Estate of Rex Whistler. All rights reserved, DACS 2008. **157** The National
Trust/Martin Trelawny **158** John Parker **159 L** © Portmeirion Ltd **R** John Parker
160-161 John Parker **162** The National Trust/John Miller **163** John Parker
164-165 The National Trust/Andrew Butler **166** © The Hall at Abbey Cwm Hir
167-168 John Parker **169** The Photolibrary Wales/Steve Benbow **170** Photograph
by permission of the University of Wales **171** Collections/Roy Shakespeare
172-173 John Parker **174** John Wynne Jones **175** John Parker **176** The National
Trust/Andrew Butler **177-179** The National Trust/Andreas von Einsiedel
180 L Alex Ramsay **180-181** The Judge's Lodging **182** John Parker
183 T CADW. Crown Copyright **B** Archie Miles **184** CADW. Crown Copyright
185 Murray Chapman

Discover Britain's Historic Houses: WALES

Reader's Digest Project Team
Series editor Christine Noble
Art editor Jane McKenna
Picture researcher Christine Hinze
Caption writer/copy editor Caroline Smith
Proofreader Ron Pankhurst
Indexer Marie Lorimer
Product production manager Claudette Bramble
Production controller Katherine Bunn

Reader's Digest General Books
Editorial director Julian Browne
Art director Anne-Marie Bulat
Managing editor Nina Hathway
Picture resource manager Sarah Stewart-Richardson
Pre-press account manager Dean Russell
Colour origination Colour Systems Limited, London
Printed and bound in Europe by Arvato, Iberia

We are committed to both the quality of our products and
the service we provide to our customers. We value your
comments, so please feel free to contact us on **08705 113366**
or via our web site at **www.readersdigest.co.uk**

If you have any comments or suggestions about the
content of our books, you can contact us at:
gbeditorial@readersdigest.co.uk

Published by The Reader's Digest Association Limited,
11 Westferry Circus, Canary Wharf, London E14 4HE

© The Reader's Digest Association Limited 2008

www.readersdigest.co.uk

This book was designed, edited and produced by The Reader's
Digest Association Limited based on material from *England's
Thousand Best Houses* by Simon Jenkins, first published by
Allen Lane, the Penguin Press, a publishing division of Penguin
Books Ltd, and on material from *Wales; Churches, Houses,
Castles*, also by Simon Jenkins and published by Allen Lane,
the Penguin Press, courtesy of Penguin Books.

Copyright © Simon Jenkins 2003 and 2008

Concept code UK0149/L/S
Book code 634-013 UP0000-1
ISBN 978 0 276 44424 1
Oracle code 356600013H.00.24